HOW TO READ THE FINANCIAL PAGES

OF YOUR NEWSPAPER

AND MUCH MORE

Revised Edition
Joseph J. Villeneuve

Published by JJV Associates

Joseph J. Villeneuve
How to Read the Financial Pages of Your Newspaper—Revised Edition
ISBN number 0-9604956-1-4

Pulished in the U.S.A. by JJV Associates
107 S. Lowell Ave.
Syracuse, N.Y. 13204

Let's Take the Mystery out of Reading the Financial Section of your Newspaper

TO THE READER

This book is intended to be an initial reference source for investors showing interest in securities in general. While great care was taken to present facts and figures which the author believes to be accurate in every detail, the book may not be entirely free of error. None of the material presented has been subjected to an independent verification.

Therefore, this book is intended to be a reference aid only, and none of the data, information, facts, or opinions contained within this book constitute representations by the author or publisher to influence action in either law or the securities industry; nor is the contents warranted to be accurate and/or complete.

Furthermore, this book is not intended to be, and should not be construed by anyone as, an offer to sell, nor as a solicitation of an offer to buy securities of any description.

ABOUT THE AUTHOR

The author has been keenly interested in sound investing practices for some 40 years. He is a prober and a student of the markets who, for some 30 years has continuously charted 40 stocks, and various market indices of the most meaningful variety which are found in the daily charts of the leading newspapers that carry New York and American Stock Exchange listings.

During the many years of investing for his own account, he was an investor among investors, and as such became aware of the lack of helpful materials of an understandable nature that is made available for beginners—the unsophisticated investors. The author has always been rather dismayed with the fact that financial organizations and the media do not always use plain understandable language when attempting to describe financial products, and just what these are designed to achieve.

For this reason the author hereby tries his hand at helping that poor Soul understand the basics of this securities industry which seems destined for tremendous growth in the years just ahead.

The author intends this work to be a good primer for potentially new investors who may want to look at the brokerage business from a Journeyman Investor's viewpoint. His acquired experience and knowledge should not be looked upon as the "last word" in the industry; but merely as a body of handy information to be "rubbed off" onto some investors who need some plain talk about securities, as opposed to the usual hard to understand security "jargon" that appears so prominently in many publications.

The author has an extensive background of 30 years in merchandising and sales promotion at the management level in department stores.

TABLE OF CONTENTS

Stock Exchange Composite Transactions
SAMPLE NEWS LISTING

Some newspapers might only display the company name, dividend, last sale, and net change from the previous day.

New Issue Since the First of the Year

Stock Split or Stock Dividend

Stock Symbols

up 1/8 From Previous Days Close

52 WEEK HIGH	LOW	STOCK		DIV.	YLD. %	P.E. RATIO	SALES 100'S	HIGH	LOW	CLOSE	NET CHG.
39 3/4	29 1/8	A.I.U. INTL	AIT	2.24	6.7	6	38	33 1/2	33	33 1/4	+1/8
24 3/4	17	AVW S	AV	.25	1.0	13	85	24 1/8	23 1/2	23 7/8	-1/8
80	57	ACCUPUNK PF	APN	2	2.9	...	5	71	70	70	...
52 7/8	51 3/4	BAYOU Wd	BOU	...	...	545	52 3/8	52	52 1/4	+1/4
19	7 5/8	BLOOPER N	BPR		1.6	11	149	18 7/8	18	18	-1/4
40	27 5/8	CAPUT INC 1.60 b	CPT		5.2	6	4	30 3/4	30 3/4	30 3/4	...
12 3/4	7 1/2	FLASH-IN-A-PAN 1.08e	FPN		12	9	31	8 7/8	8 7/8	8 7/8	+1/8

Preferred Stock

When Distributed

b Indicates Annual Rate Plus Stock Dividend

e - Declared or Paid in Preceding 12 Months

Stock Market Quotation Explanations

High-Low:
Currently the high-low figures on the extreme left of a stock quotation column reflect the high and low prices of the latest 52 weeks up to but not including the previous day.

Stock Name:
The names of stocks are usually abbreviated for purposes of conserving space. Some listings will display stock symbols following the names for easy access to data bases.

Highly abbreviated stocks which cannot be found in regular alphabetical order, should be found listed at the top of that alphabet column.

Dividends
This column generally carries the regular annual per-share dividend as of the last quarter or semi-annual declaration. (unless otherwise noted) .

Stock's Sales In 100's
This column carries the number of round lots. A round lot consists of 100 shares. Occasionally certain stocks will be listed **in full** as opposed to **100**

share lots in some newspapers. When this happens a designation such as Z will be inserted next to the volume of sales listed and the letter such as Z will be " keyed" to the explanatory notes, not to mislead the reader.

High:

This is a high for a particular stock traded on the given day.

Low:

This is the lowest price which a stock traded on the given day.

The high-low figures for a given day are important to traders because they show the volatility of the market in a particular stock on any given day. The difference between the high and low is referred to in the industry as the "spread".

Close:

This is the price at which a stock is traded in the last transaction of the day. The importance of the "close" to a trader is in giving him some idea where the stock may resume trading on the next day.

Net Chg:

Net change calls attention to the difference between the closing price on the preceding business day and the current day.

Yield %:

Yield percent has to do with the percentage of return on one's investment in a stock. This is simply obtained by dividing today's current closing price of a stock into the annual dividend. Putting this another way, yield percent will tell you what sort of a return you can expect to get on your invested money in a particular stock on the basis of the dividend as it refers to that day's closing price.

P.E. Ratio:

Price earnings ratio or (P.E. Ratio) is a very simple way of showing the current yearly earnings and has nothing to do with dividends.

By dividing the P.E. Ratio figure into the current market price, one gets the dollar earnings per share.

Example—on a day when a stock sells at $60.00 a share and carries a price earnings ratio of 15, the indicated earnings would be $4.00 a share—by dividing 15 into $60.00.

The P.E. Ratio is used greatly as a tool to determine **relative value**. Stocks carrying the P.E. Ratio of 20 to one, might also be referred to as selling at twenty times earnings. There is no precise price-to-earnings ratio that can be classified as a good value. P.E. Ratios are all relative to many factors in the market place, but some factors carry far more weight than others in how they affect current market values of stocks. Economic factors, market and mass psychology, technological developments in companies and industrial groups, along with the relative proficiency of management teams would be considered some of the more important elements which **determine value.**

Stock Price Increments:

All stock prices on U.S. auction markets listed in newspapers are expressed in 1/8th increments of a dollar, or 12 1/2¢ increments. These are recorded on the tables as 1/8-1/4-3/8-1/2-5/8-3/4 and 7/8. For example a stock price of 50 1/8 on the tables would actually be a price of $50.12 1 /2, 50 1/4 would be$50.25, 50 3/8 would be $50.37 1/2, 50 1/2 would be $50.50, 50 5/8 would be $50.62 1/2, 50 3/4 would be expressed as $50.75 and 50 7/8 would be read as $50.87 1/2.

Shareholder:

A shareholder purchases a stock certificate through his brokerage which makes him a part owner (or shareholder) in a company.

Generally speaking there are 2 classes of stock consisting of the common and the preferred stocks.

Preferred stockholders receive dividends ahead of the common stockholders who have no such preference order, but the common shareholders dividend may be paid, lowered, increased, or entirely omitted based on the judgment of the board of directors as they view the corporations ability to pay dividends based on current earnings. This is not to say that preferred dividends may not also be skipped over. The cumulative preferreds having dividends in arrears have to be paid before common dividends can be declared.

Conservative investors tend to view preferred stocks as they would bonds in so far as they are a senior security which generally has an attractive fixed annual dividend rate. The preferreds as in the case of bonds can be "called," but are next in line after the bonds in the corporation's order of legal payments.

Long Sale:

The simple procedure of buying a stock outright.

Short Sale:

When an investor sells a stock which he does not own in anticipation that he will buy back the same stock at a lower price, and deliver the shares back to the lender, thereby showing a profit.

Bull:

A trader who has purchased securities or commodities expecting that these will rise in value. Having bought he becomes a prospective seller.

Bear:
One who expects to buy securities at lower price levels. This investor may sell short in a declining market, in which case he becomes a prospective buyer at lower levels when he "covers" to replace the borrowed stock.

Cover:
Buying a security that previously had been sold short - thereby replacing the borrowed stock.

Dividend:
That portion of earnings that a company will pay stockholders as a return on his investment in the company.

Growth Stocks:
These are shares of firms that show a steady climb in gross earnings, and which use a substantial portion of the net profit for expansion, research, or development.

Hot Issues:
These are generally new issues of common stocks which are coming onto the market at a price considered by speculators to be below real potential value.

Gilt Edged:
This term is used to indicate securities of the highest quality.

Odd Lot:
This is an amount of stock that is less than the established unit of trading on an exchange. (or less than 100 shares)

In And Out:
An "in and outer" is one who buys and sells securities in a short period of time.

Round Turn, or Round Trip:
The term simply refers to the process of having completed the purchase and the sale of the same security.

Treasury Stock:
These are shares of stock which having been originally issued as outstanding stock, are later reacquired by the corporation. This stock receives no dividends or voting rights while it is being held by the corporation. This treasury stock may be resold, retired, or held indefinitely.

Prime Rate:
The interest rate that banks may charge the largest borrowers having the best credit standings.

Discount Rate:
This is the interest rate that the Federal Reserve Bank will charge for loans to member commercial banks. This rate changes with conditions in the

money market, and is raised or lowered by the Fed. whenever it believes bank credit should be tightened or loosened. This rate greatly affects general interest rates.

Commissions:
These are broker's charges to an investor or client for acting as an agent in the purchasing or selling of securities or other property.

Exchange Specialist:
Typically, the specialist's job is to process buy or sell orders given to him by commission brokers on behalf of investors. The totality of these orders constitute his "book". The orders are executed in the market when a security reaches the price specified in the customer's order. The specialist acting as dealer buys or sells for his own account thus provid ing depth and continuity in efforts to maintain stability in the prices of his assigned stocks. The specialist may also handle odd-lot orders that come onto the trading floor of the exchange.

Seat:
This refers to a broker's membership on a security exchange.

Street:
This is a popular reference to Wall Street's financial district in New York City.

Federal Reserve Board:
This is the quasi-government agency that controls the supply of and price of currencies, regulates installment credit rates, and margin loans.

Balance Sheet
A statement showing the nature and amount of a firm's assets, liabilities, and capital structure on a given date.

Earnings Report:
This statement of income, also called the profit-loss statement shows the earnings or losses over a specific time span.

This report lists all income items earned, expenses incurred, and net profit resulting from operations.

Equity-Issue-Stock:
Words used to describe ownership interest in common or preferred stock-holders in a company.

Investment Banker:
A company that underwrites the issuing to the investing public of new securities by a corporation.

Proxy:
A written authorization from a stockholder describing to the corporate officers how the stockholder wishes to cast his or her vote at a shareholder's meeting that he or she cannot attend.

Liquidity:

When many investors are buying and selling a stock, the issue is said to be liquid—providing opportunity for ready dealing. The wide opposite is found in the il-liquid real estate market where bids vary widely based on people's wide and varying perceptions of value.

Rate of Return:

The rate of return on a stock is calculated in terms of the dividend. A stock purchased at $100 that pays a yearly dividend of $6 would effectively yield 6% as a rate of return.

Volatility:

The value of any investment can change. Volatility measures the **speed** and **breadth** of that change.

Inflation Risk:

When the return on an investment isn't larger than the rate of inflation, the investor "winds up" with more money, but worse off because the dollars are only worth what they may buy.

Diversification:

The strategy of spreading one's investments over several securities to reduce one's exposure to **excessive risk**.

Have insurmountable problems?
Contact the **Arbitration Department** of the New York Stock Exchange at 11 Wall Street, New York, N.Y. 10005——or the National Association of Securities Dealers, at 2 World Trade Center, New York, N.Y. 10048.

Types Of Orders

Market Order:

An order with a broker to buy immediately at the prevailing market price is called a "market order."

Limit Order:

A "limit order" is one instructing the broker to put a limit on what price the customer is willing to pay for a stock.

Day Order:

A "day order" is exactly what it means, good for a day only.

GTC Order:

The "GTC order" is one that is good until executed or cancelled by the investor.

Stock Table Footnotes

Footnotes: These are the symbols (or letters) which follow the name of a stock on the stock quotation tables. They are keyed to the following list of fine print footnotes which appear at the bottom of a quotation page. These footnotes are generally carried in all papers that give extensive to complete coverage of the stock tables.

PF - Indicates a preferred issue of stock.

WT - Indicates a warrant which is a right or privilege given a stockholder to buy shares of a new issue at a preferential price which will most probably be lower than the stock's price when it hits the market.

A - Also extra or extras — generally refers to an extra dividend which has been declared over and above the indicated annual rate.

B - Annual rate plus stock dividend — indicates that a cash and a stock dividend is declared annually.

C - Liquidating dividend — firm is going out of business, has sold assets, and this is part of, or may represent the final distribution to stockholders.

E - Declared or paid in preceding 12 months. Used when a stated annual dividend has not been in effect.

I - Declared or paid after stock dividend or split-up. Dividend declared for the new shares after the stock has been split. For example 2 for 1 or 3 for 1. Dividend would most probably be smaller than the old dividend.

J - Paid this year, dividend omitted, deferred or no action taken at last dividend meeting. Would possibly indicate that the firm is conserving its cash for other purposes, or has fallen on hard times and is unable to pay the usual dividend.

K - Declared or paid this year, an accumulative issue with dividends in arrears. This would most probably concern a cumulative preferred stock.

R - Declared or paid in preceding 12 months plus stock dividend. This would indicate that an extra consisting of a stock dividend was declared during the last 12 months.

T - Paid in stock in preceding 12 months, estimated cash value on ex-dividend or ex-distribution date.

X - Ex-dividend or ex-rights — if one buys a stock on the day it carries the

"X" designation, one will not be entitled to the recently declared dividend. It takes 5 trading days before the name of the new owner of stock will appear on the books of the corporation as an owner. The previous owner gets the dividend during ex-dividend 5 days. Ex-rights refers to the "rights" to subscribe to additional company shares.

Y - Ex-dividend and sales in full. (already explained)

Z - Sales in full — indication is that the sales of stock are not reported in round lots, (or 100 share lots) but are quoted in the exact amount of shares traded.

CLD - Called— as in the case of a preferred stock which is called back by a corporation to save on further dividend payments, or to convert them to common stock having lower dividend payments.

WI - When issued—to indicate trading in a new stock issue which has been announced but not yet issued.

WW - With warrants — a new issue which carries with it warrants as an inducement, possibly to turn in the old stock in a reorganization effort. Also, in the case of the financing of a new issue, warrants might also be issued as a "sweetener" inducement intended to help the sales marketing effort of the new issue.

XW - Without warrants — just the opposite of "WW."

VI - In bankruptcy, receivership, or being reorganized under the Bankruptcy Act, or securities assumed by such companies.

U - Indicates a new 52 week high.

D - Indicates a new 52 week low.

S - Stock split or stock dividend amounting to 25% or more since Jan. 1. The 52 week high-low range and dividend begin with the date of the split or stock dividend, and does not cover the entire 52 week period.

G - Dividends or earnings in Canadian money. Stock trades in U.S. dollars. No yield, or P.E. shown unless stated in U.S. money.

N - New issue in the past 52 weeks. The 52 week high/low range begins when trading starts in the new issue.

WD - When distributed.

V - Trading halted on the Primary market.

RT - Rights.

UN - Units.

Yld - Stands for yield, or the percentage of return represented by the annual dividend at the current stock price.

SELF HELP-- BY DOING IT YOURSELF

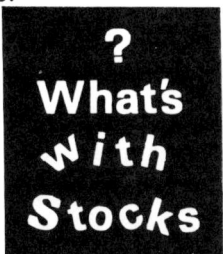

There are many books and financial publications available to the general public in the country's libraries that are kept up-dated and which provide valuable sources of needed information. The larger county libraries subscribe to numerous expensive national **financial data books** that are kept current and which may help an investor in developing his or her own investment strategy. Whether one is dealing in stocks, bonds, or mutual funds, one may find a wealth of current statistics from these volumes in a **library business department**. Many colleges will offer low cost courses on the basics of investing.

Those people who are interested in dealing with **discounts brokers** will definitely save on **commissions**, buy these people surely must do their **homework.** They should perhaps subscribe to one or two financial mags, and they should also be reading the financial section of a good newspaper on a regular basis. Also, a great help may result from being placed on the mailing list of the various industrial and commercial companies in which one has developed an interest, to receive the annual and quarterly reports etc. These will be mailed by most firms free of charge for the asking, by contacting the **investor contact person**, or the company **secretary**. Names and addresses are listed on every Standard & Poor's Corp. stock report found in the **financial section** of your **library**.

The fascination about annual stock reports if there is any at all, is to compare the **newest reports** against the **old ones**. Brokers can also help their clients receive annual reports. These reports will normally contain a statement of the company's earnings compared with its **past performance**. The report will also discuss the possible introduction of new products or procedures, and will present an overview of industrial relations as needed.

BE AN
INFORMED
AND
AWARE
INVESTOR

The progress or deterioration of a company may very often be ascertained by merely reading the chief operating officer's **annual** or **quarterly** report **message** to the stockholders. Do his remarks indicate positive progress? Do his remarks show that he's "fluffing" over the important disappointing results with the sort of verbiage that only amounts to "throwing the bull"? Does the chairman's obsevations on the other hand frankly detail that the company has some **serious problems** to solve, and does he seem to have a bold **concrete plan** to get the job done? Having a "nose" to sense an impending correction in a company is sometimes the **key** to a stock that is about to "hatch" an **improvement** worth many dollars to a participating investor.

Detecting what is corporate **puffery** as opposed to the **straight facts** by comparing the tone of the annual and quarterly reports against previous reports should prove beneficial to the investor. Therefore, the "soaking-up" of all the information one can relative to your strategy and the mechanics of investing as noted in the above remarks may be time well spent, and if investors are able to achieve a good degree of **fine-tuning** of their experience, they are ready for discount brokers, and perhaps may do without the services of **full service brokers**. Investors may also get to realize that it's not a good idea to get too "far-a-field" with research; but to concentrate on getting all the information they can on the companies whose stock they find interesting, not to mention the need to follow the activities of those shares that are already owned by the investors.

DO YOU KNOW WHAT THE CURRENT AND LONG-TERM "BEST PERFORMERS" ARE?

HOW BIG A JOB IS THIS?

YOU SHOULD!

The job of investing may be a minor one, or it may become a full time job. If an investor owns three to five investment grade long-term conservative growth stocks or conservative bond funds, the job is fairly easy, and it's more or less a patient waiting game as the investor follows the activities of the firms, and the action of the securities on whatever exchange they are listed. This is not too exciting (like watching a cactus grow), and would be downright boring to an active trader. However, this is perhaps one of the **surest** ways of investing and not **losing** one's capital.

The average investor on the other hand who owns three to five businessman's speculation stocks for a short to intermediate profit, needs to follow them very closely, as these stocks may fluctuate at the markets in response to **technical** and **whimsical** reasons. The average investor will find this a doable job, but should perhaps not get in any deeper unless he or she is highly sophisticated **Wall Street-wise**.

On the other hand, can you just visualize yourself owning 20 to 30 growth or speculative stocks? You would now have a **full time job** on your hands that requires very close supervision of the portfolio. This is a situation in which a dedicated and vigilant broker can be of **measurable help** to the client, by keeping in tough once or twice a week as needed — this, to discuss maintenance of the account, and any fast breaking market news relating to the investor's stock on hand. The average investor should not of course be so heavily committed, as the trading of 20 to 30 stocks on a continuous basis for capital gains is job for a very nimble investor who is **well versed** in the world of investments, and who can work **full time** on the requirements of the portfolio. This type of portfolio normally requires many **round-trips** into the market, and the results of the trades do not always represent the **capital gains** that the investor is seeking to achieve. There are **losses** on trades which must at times be taken to prevent the occurrence of deeper losses.

The speculative trader tries to operate in such a way that his profits on trades together with any accumulated dividends will more than **offset** the **trading**

DON'T ALWAYS TRY TO HIT
"HOME RUNS"
TRY HITTING SINGLES AND
DOUBLES

losses. The average investor finds it comparatively easy to buy into a security—"like getting married". This same investor would in many cases find it difficult to know when to sell—"like getting a divorce".

The nimble trader though, has a predetermined selling point, and when his stock prices reach this flash point he perhaps sells out with the same **greed** and **determination** that typifies his approach to the entire trading arena. The trader looks dispassionately upon his stock certificates as **mere products** to be bought and sold, thereby hopefully achieving a profit that more than offsets the corrosive effect that **monetary inflation** has upon his invested capital.

The wise investor is the informed investor who tries to clearly understand what each investment is all about, how it is structured, whether or not it fits into his or her investment strategy, and tries to evaluate the **risks** as opposed to the possible benefits.

One should always bear in mind that the individual's stature is microscopic relative to the markets. The big "movers" and "shakers" in the markets are the **moneyed institutions** that realize they are in a world where **time** is **money**, and speed pays off big. These institutions employ financial experts and services many of which have access to **computerized trading** with highly sophisticated strategies.

This is the kind of competitive setting in which an individual investor finds himself as he or she trades from his or her own available information. However, one should **not despair** of one's chance for success, because the forces of supply, demand, credit, and psychology that propel the market are even greater than the institutions. The indivdiual investor with a limited commitment to a limited portfolio may trade with **more ease**, and tailor the portfolio **much easier** than the heavily commited institutions that are trading in **big blocks** of individual stock. (much easier to trade 300 than 10,000 shares)

MAKE YOUR SECURITY TRADES ON THE SOUND APPLICATION OF FACTS - NOT EMOTION.

PRICES:

The price of nearly everything in the world is determined by **supply and demand** with securities being no different. The main ingredients that propel supply and demand of shares are generally **earnings** and **dividends** per share. What is really meaningful to the prices of an ongoing firm would be its **earning power** and its growth potential. The price on the stock of a **new company** that is just starting up, could be related closely to the value of the **assets** which initially make up its net worth. However, once the company is in operation, the factors most likely to control the stock price would be **supply** (bids) and **demand** (asked price).

These two factors have to do with distribution and accumulation. Distribution is the **selling process** that goes on when stocks that have been accumulated by investors and traders at low price levels, are then sold when the issues have risen substantially. In many cases, distribution tends to have a **negative impact** on the market. Likewise, the prices of an entire market will **go soft** when there is general distribution (sell off). Accumulation, on the other hand, occurs when institutions, investors, and professional traders start a **process** of **accumulating** stocks to add to their holdings. This phenomenon is generally considered to be **positive** for the health of the market.

The assets of a company aren't worth a "plugged nickle" if they don't have **earning power.** If plants, machinery and equipment at an industrial firm are not working to produce earnings, they have a **minus value**, which is the cost of removing the plant to make room for another plant that will generate earnings.

Some people tend to think that a $10.00 a share stock is inferior to a $25.00 a share stock. This is not necessarily the case.

This crude example will help to illustrate that the price of a stock has a **relationship** to the number of shares outstanding: let's assume that company A and company B both have assets of $100,000,000. Company A however has but 4,000,000 shares outstanding whereas company B has 10,000,000 shares outstanding to the general public. By dividing the 4 million shares of company A into the 100 million dollars of net worth, we come up with a basic value of $25.00 per share. Also, by dividing the 10 million shares into the 100 million net worth of company B, we arrive at a $10.00 per share of basic net worth.

Market price will tend to relate to the **basic price**, but will actually be determined by the **consensus** of what some investors will be willing to give on any given day for a specific stock, and what another group of investors will be **willing to accept** for this stock. When these diverse groups of people having directly opposed perceptions of what a security is worth come to a **meeting of the minds** — we then have a market. It all "boils down" to what one investor will pay for a stock that another is willing to sell.

If the net worth of company A shown above falls on hard times, and has to dissipate 50% of its assets through some competitive crunch or other malfunction, investors will be quick to recognize this; and will perhaps **discount** the basic value of this $25.00 stock to $12.50 or less. The market value would then be more or less than $12.50, again, depending on the consensus value placed by the various investors at the stock markets, reacting, as they would to company A's asset problems.

The **size** of a company and the **price** of its stock does not necessarily make it a better value. We have seen some of the **giants** of industry go "belly up" into chapter seven and eleven **bankruptcy** in recent years. We've seen companies so laden with debt, that despite owning millions in assets they were forced, because of their **negative net worth,** to go into bankruptcy to satisfy the **creditors** and lending banks.

When a stock sells cheap relative to its usual higher level, there's generally a **good reason** for it cheapness. The reasons could be bad management, a weak competitive posture vis-a-vis the company's competitors, or financial problems, like carrying too much debt. A company could also be **legislated** out of business, such as the result of what happened when the country became aware that the environment was **being impacted** by the asbestos producers, and some chemical companies. There's a host of other problems too numerous to mention here that could cause a stock to plummet into near oblivion.

The two big questions which seem to plague the average investors are, **when to buy,** and at what **level** do they sell. The human emotions being as

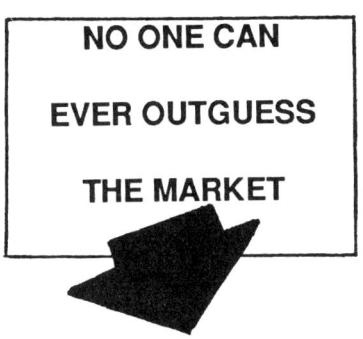

NO ONE CAN

EVER OUTGUESS

THE MARKET

they are (selfish), the tendency is for some investors to try selling at the **top** of the market, and to buy at the bottom. This is perhaps foolhardy, because there's no foolproof way to detect the exact top of an ascending market, or the exact **bottom** of a decending one. If a person had the answer to that informational (gem), he or she could make a "big pot" of money **several times** during their lifetime.

The studying of **market trends** therefore becomes important. Knowing where the market stands in a business cycle is perhaps very necessary for good investors and speculators. It's not at all important that an investor's timing to buy or sell be **so precise** as to hit the **top** of a market in his or her trading efforts. No one knows what the exact top or bottom of a market will be; so, trying to buy or sell at prices within a 15% to 20% **range** of those two **extremities** would be considered good investment practice by many knowledgeable investors.

The really large profits from market operations are made by those who have the courage to buy-in when everything is at its darkest; when comparatively speaking, stock trading volume has dried up and everything seems to be trading in a **narrow range**, with price to earnings ratios **very low** (like three to four times earnings), and the outlook for the economy is horrendous. What manner of fool would buy into this sort of depressingly harsh economy? It's those of course who realize that the **next major trend** will be on the upside — the **bulls**.

The buying of low priced stocks when nobody else seemed to want them, has in the past rewarded many investors who have had the staying power and patience to stay with stocks during the **low volume doldrums** that preceeds the emergence of another bull market.

Toward the upper ranges of a bull market the craziness seems to be just as bad. A type of **euphoric mania** seems to drive investors into a bidding competition for owning stocks. When these excesses grind to a halt, the traditional bears are not alone. The bulls, driven by a sudden surge of mass

psychology to get out and realize their profit, will automatically become bears. When this happens, a crisis of major magnitude takes place that breaks the **speculative bubble**, and a selling stampede ensues incontrollably; whereby everyone is a seller, and there are no buyers. This type of market scenario will often **portend the end** of a bull market such as the country experienced on October 19th and 20th of 1987.

When such a market disaster occurs, the good stocks go down nearly as far, and as fast as the cats and dogs. None of the participants is saved, the angels and the sinners will **both get hurt**, and the (angels) good paying dividend stocks will perhaps be beaten down almost as badly as those sleazy glamourous issues. The important job then, will be finding those issues that will **recover soonest** when an atmosphere of normalcy returns to the markets. This means that smart investors will go back to **basics**, avoiding investments in companies that have heavy debt burdens, that have excessively high price/earnings ratios (those above 10), and the sharp investor will also tend to insulate himself against buying stocks, the touted expectations of which do not **measure up** to current realities.

Following a major market breakdown, many investors turn to the **money market funds** to park their monies while awaiting better times — not a **bad strategy** for the average investor. During bad times the banks make a good play for your extra dollars. They will often give you a gift for opening an account. Many investors will then place their money in bank certificates of deposit, especially if the interest rates are decent at the time.

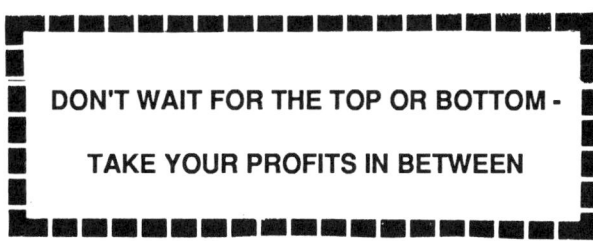

DON'T WAIT FOR THE TOP OR BOTTOM -

TAKE YOUR PROFITS IN BETWEEN

INVESTOR FEARS:

All stock market eras have their strengths and weaknesses from which investors draw upon for their fears or bullish optimism. We're currently in a time of cautious pessimism, if not downright fear, insofar as the average investor is concerned.

The crash of October 19th and 20th of 1987 is our **latest culprit.** Investors just can't dream themselves out of that stock-market crash, even after the Wall Street reforms that followed, and were intended to **reassure investors** in the aftermath of that dreadful market tumble. Here we are eighteen months after the crash and surveys seem to indicate that the majority of individual investors think that the stock market presents **more risk today** than it did before the crash. These are times when investors are placing more of their monies in bank accounts and money market funds to avoid the **pitfalls** of another crash.

Bad memories are difficult to erase, and at times like these the Over-the-Counter Market takes a real beating. The small investors play an important role in this Over-the-Counter Market, and their **nervousness** at this point is very high after being successful in the **five year** period prior to October 19, 1987.

This investors' loss of confidence in the stability of stocks has created a sagging market volume-wise that has been **devastating** for the brokerage business. Prior to the October 19th disaster the volume of trading reported on the Big Board was very consistantly in the area of 170 million shares to 200 million shares per day. Many of these trading days even exceeded the 200 million shares per day, as the market in all its foward looking optimism heated up toward the well **remembered disaster**.

Be aware
that during your
lifetime
there will be
five or six
great opportunities
for profit

Today, a year and a half later, the average big board volume ranges in the area of 110 million to 150 million shares, with only an occasional 200 million share day. Stockbroker trades for investors are reported to be down 28% from pre-crash levels. Many brokerage companies had geared their expenses to those **200 million share days**, and when volume became badly depressed they were stunned, and had to quickly cut expenses which many did by instituting substantantial **layoffs** of employees and through the **attrition** process.

This shifting of many brokerage customers from the bullish stance of pre-Oct. 19th, to a wait-and-see attitude has been a **shocker** for the brokerage industry. These current customers seem to be investing only in securities which they feel very comfortable with. The majority of these customers find it increasingly more difficult to have **solid confidence** in a broker's advice.

Sensing this lack of customer confidence, the brokerage business then embarked on an advertising campaign with a **highly conservative bias.** Their theme of course was to tout securities of a more **dependable nature**, hoping in this way to restore their stock clientel's confidence which they, the brokerages, so sorely needed to remain **solvent**. The few brokerage firms that were unable to remain solvent after the shock treatment of October 19, 1987 were forced to **merge** into the stronger of the species.

One must understand that brokerage people have two main sources of income: one is derived from client commissions and one is obtained by trading securities for their own account. The commission generated customer business is what enables a brokerage firm to survive in the **high rent district** and maintain a sound service organization. When the brokerages lose their customer following, it's time to grab their hats and lock the door; because the party is over.

While most brokerage firms have survived the **negative impact** of Black Monday, the fact remains that over 80% of their customers firmly believe that Stock-Index Options trading and futures trading have made it far more difficult for customers to understand (as the song would say) what **goes on behind** those closed doors. This of course refers to the **illiquidity** which seems to be caused by the Super Dot program trading system that initiates **drastic gyrations** in trading, which in turn is perhaps mainly responsible for great upheavals in prices, or serious downturns in prices.

Security customers view this sort of trading madness with great apprehension and **mistrust** of the system. Indications are such that, a year and a half after the devastation of Black Monday, investors are placing **very little trust** in even the best of stock market savants. Investors at this point in time are doing much more of their own thinking, and accepting less advice from stockbrokers.

We don't want to be unkind by **bashing stockbrokers** too badly, but if you have reservations concerning yours, why not test your broker. Do it this way. Arm yourself with solid information concerning a leading stock, and especially on the recent developments which are occurring at the company. Then, ask your broker leading questions concerning this stock. If he's **serious** about helping, you'll perhaps find that he's not prepared to answer these queries. Naturally, you **can't expect** your broker to know everything about every stock. He'll perhaps want to call back to you with the answer. However, you may want to **avoid a broker** who has a smart off the cuff answer to your every question. This broker is "winging it" and would perhaps fail your test. He's the type who **doesn't want to help** with your research. He's strickly a "fast buck" order taker who should be avoided, unless of course he's a discount broker.

In this type of environment, all of the outside tentacles of the markets such as: timing services, privately published financial news letters, and independent investment counselors all have their **discomfort problems** "staying afloat". The name of the game for these investment services is to **survive** this period of stock market malaise. The newsletters rely heavily on direct-mail solicitations to investors. They do well in good times market-wise by soliciting subscriptions to their newsletters from the thousands of small investors who are eager to participate in the touted opportunities for stock profits.

Post-crash, however, the costs of planning, printing and mailing this newsletter literature becomes **mighty expensive** when few people respond. Post-crash response rates of newsletter direct-mail solicitations are reported to have fallen "out of bed", like 50% lower than the responses that they received from their **pre-crash mailings.**

Some of the well known newsletters are doing quite well, especially if they were in the elite group who's gurus advised their clients pre-crash to **reduce** their **stock exposure** with perceptive discrimination. However, since the crash, most newsletters are suffering for lack of business. This is a temporary phenomenon, and the newsletters will again have their "come back" when they again have something that's **believable** for their subscribers.

**Never! Never!
go partners with anyone
in stock market trades.**

DIVIDENDS:

The dividend is the amount of money paid to the investor who owns stock in a company. This amount of cash is usually **paid the investor** in cash, but may at times be paid in stock, or in both stock and cash. The dividend is a payment of that part of a company's earnings determined to be net profit, and therefore available for payment to stockholders. The other part of a company's **earnings** will generally be used for current working capital, expenses, and if necessary the acquiring of additional assets, which may help to **increase** its **financial base**.

Dividends are distinct from an interest payment. The interest is money received for the use (or rental of money); such as bank interest or bond interest. Interest is money paid as a result of an I.O.U. of some sort, and not the result of corporate ownership. The dividends of most companies are paid on a **regular basis** every three months, but they may also be paid twice a year, or even annually. Some are paid at irregular times, and the amount and times are **decided separately** every year.

Some corporations are very **scrupulous** about paying the same amount, or even an increased amount of dividends regularly. Many investors buy the securities of such companies for this very good reason. When a corporation is undergoing growing pains, or in real financial trouble, it will very often **reduce** the dividend or **withhold** it completely, in order to perhaps meet a competitive challenge, increase its asset base to improve its earnings; or again the company might "husband" its cash to possibly **cope** with its **financial problems.**

In such cases where all the profits are being **retained** for company use, and no dividend is declared, the stockholders' only chance to benefit would perhaps be through a **capital gain** of their share prices. The shareholders in such a situation would naturally hope that this reinvestment of profit dollars would help to position the company for **further growth**, that would ultimately result in increased profit, and the resumption of **dividend payments.**

The elected board of directors will be the team deciding whether to "squirrel" away the dividend for internal use or pay dividends — generally on a quarterly time table based on the company **earnings**, its current long term **obligations**, and future plans relative to **expansion.**

When things go wrong with a company, and the dividend is reduced or eliminated, and perhaps the price of the stock drops dramatically, there's perhaps nothing that will "wake-up" a **complacent stockholder** more quickly than this event. He wonders what's happening, what he must do, and what are **his rights.**

STOCKHOLDERS' RIGHTS:

The stockholders have many rights, and many are not even aware of these rights. These privileges depend in some measure on the **regulations** of the state in which the company is incorporated. The stockholder, upon buying stock, acquires the right to share in the **corporation's profits** if the directors see their way clear to declare the dividends. Through the **proxy**, he has the right to elect the company directors. He has a right to receive annual and quarterly **reports** detailing the company finances and earnings. He has a right to inspect the books of his company, to vote on any **mergers** or **consolidations**, and also to vote on any suggested changes in the charter of incorporation. In some states, stockholders have preemptive rights to buy new securities when they become available.

Stockholders have the right to hold the **directors responsible** for their stewardship — by legal means if they want to go that route.

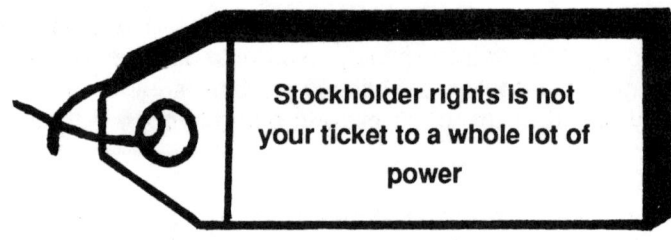

Stockholder rights is not your ticket to a whole lot of power

Small stockholders will find that, thinking in practical terms, some of these rights are not **exactly powers**. An example is the right to throw out the management team that consists of the officers and directors. This is done by way of the **proxy fight** when certain large stockholders are "fed-up" with the status quo and want the top "rascals" out. It takes a lot of votes to **fire management,** but when enough of the professional investors, such as banks, investment trusts, mutual funds, and insurance companies get together with their **large blocks** of a company's stock, they can perhaps muster the voting power needed to **retire management** and seize control of the company. These are the people who do **understand** the issues involved, and having a great deal of money invested, they actively and **intensively analyze** the earnings and the operations of the companies in which they have **active investments**.

Therefore, unless there is a well orchestrated **power base** in favor of a removal attempt, it's entirely unrealistic to believe that the thousands of stockholders have the power to remove the directors .

A small stockholder is not in a position to act on such matters, or even to know how to act. The small stockholder can only **evaluate** both sides of the proxy issue, and hope that he's correctly voting his proxy. Many stockholders not only lack the basic understanding of the issues involved, but, may also lack the **capacity** and **energy** to "size-up" the performance of their management team intelligently, and from a **critical** viewpoint.

Share owners may also sue officers and directors for gross mismanagement, fraud, dishonesty, and **misuse** of their powers as officers. Last but not least — as a stockholder, you may **throw yourself out**, by selling your stock. At this point you're resigning from the company, and of course you cease to be an owner.

When stock markets act bullish, many investors buy stock for **capital appreciation** rather than the incidental dividends. However, when the bull market stalls and capital gains all but disappear, investor interest again returns for many people to the strategy of **accumulating dividends**. When the big Wall Street firms are again touting good conservative dividend paying stocks, you'll know that the spirit of the market place has returned to **calmer**, more **realistic**, and more healthy times.

Some smart investors never lose their interest in good dividend yields. The dividend **accumulators** know that over the long run they may perhaps make more money accumulating dividends bit by bit, than others might in **stock price appreciation**; only to lose the entire "pot" in sharply fluctuating markets.

The dividend reinvestment plans of various companies have contributed great wealth over the years to those who have participated on a consistant basis — **reinvesting** their dividends which tend to **compound** their earnings. When this takes place, the dividends that are reinvested begin to earn **dividends themselves**.

Over the last 30 to 40 years **dividends** have contributed 40% of an investor's total earnings of the good companies. The remaining 60% of an investor's earnings would have come from the **price appreciation** of the stock. This is like saying that the investor who ignores dividends is in a 60% **part time endeavor**. Ignoring dividend activity jibes with much of the public's current attitude, that a stock purchased in the **morning** should show a price increase by **afternoon**. That's a whole lot to expect — from greed.

```
┌■■■■■■■■┐
■              ■
■  HAVE A SOUND AND  ■
■              ■
■  PRUDENT PLAN FOR  ■
■              ■
■  YOUR MONIES.      ■
■              ■
└■■■■■■■■┘
```

SAFEKEEPING OF
STOCK CERTIFICATES:

The tangible evidence of stock ownership is the stock certificate. All stock transactions on a stock exchange culminates in a stock certificate being issued to the **registered owner**. The brokerage handling the transactions will adhere to the investor's wishes by either having the stocks registered in the investor's name, or by causing them to be registered in "street name", which is Wall Street's idiom, indicating that the stocks are registered in the **brokerage company's name.**

The internal **bookkeeping** at the broker's firm, along with the broker's **monthly statements**, provide ample evidence of customer ownership when stocks are kept in "street name".

There are certain **advantages**, depending on the investor's needs, of carrying securities in "street name". The stocks in a safe deposit vault or under your mattress (God forbid!) are not automatically **insured**. However, those stocks in street name are federally insured by the **SIPC program** up to $500,000, and the excess insurance coverage carried by a brokerage firm might bring an individual investor's coverage up to $10,000,000. If you want to trade on **margin,** (credit), your securities have to be in **"street name"** to provide adequate **collateral** for the brokerage firm.

People who hold their own certificates often lose track of their stock or bond prices; whereas those securities held in street name become the source of brokers' monthly statements that provide recent prices by which the investor may monitor his or her investments. This is perhaps done **more effectively** of course by reviewing the stock or bond quotes of a good daily or weekly **newspaper**.

When your stocks are kept in "street name" your dividends are collected and credited to your account automatically. So is the interest on your money. There's no **time lost** in collecting interest on your monies.

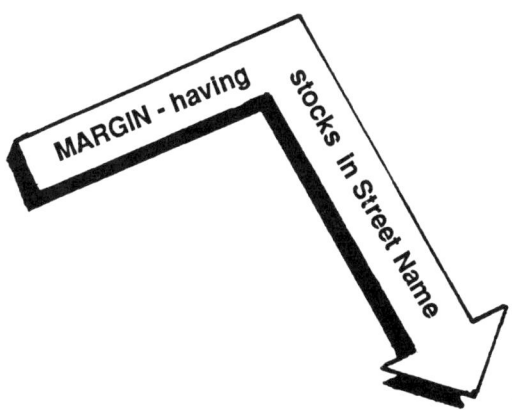

MARGIN - having stocks in Street Name

Also, if you want to trade your stocks, **a simple phone call** will accomplish this if your broker is in **possession** of your stocks. You then forego the hassel of having to locate your certificates, whether they are at home or in a bank safe deposit box, and get them to your broker within the **five business days** required by the industry.

If one resides in the Eastern states, and is buying a stock through a San Francisco or a Los Angeles broker, one would have to send a check to the broker on the **trade date**, in order to assure that the broker received payment within the five days allowed to finalize the trade. The same would apply on a sale — the **stock certificate** should be mailed out **certified mail** on the trade date when coast to coast mailing is involved. If the account is in "street name", the broker of course has possession of the certificates and this makes it that much easier for the investor.

There are various **disadvantages** to keeping certificates in "street name". Owners of these securities in brokers' hands should make it a regular practice to check the brokers' statements for **errors** or **omissions**. When errors are found the brokerage should be notified by letter. Always keep a copy of these communications; so, in looking back, if necessary, you'll know what transpired by **your copies** of all documentations. The follow through on some errors may take some time, patience, and persistence to correct— so stay with the problem until it's corrected. **Don't** rely on **phone calls** to correct errors found in a monthly statement from your broker. Put your gripe in a **letter** and keep a copy just in case it later becomes necessary to reconstruct the events that transpired.

**ALL STOCKS ARE
BOUGHT TO BE SOLD**

Another disadvantage of keeping stocks in "street name" arises from the practice of the brokers not getting company information out to the investor. Annual and quarterly reports as well as company progress letters may be held by the brokerage, and may never be mailed out to the investor. If mailed, they may arrive late. This **lessens** the individual's **control** over his or her investments. Also, under these conditions, brokers receive and **vote proxy statements**, causing you the shareholder to **lose your** decision making **imput** with your selected company. You also **forego** your opportunity to share in your company's Dividend Reinvestment Program.

In the improbable event that your brokerage company declared bankruptcy, your stocks held with the broker would most likely be "frozen" for several months during which time you could not dispose of your securities — **not a pleasant thought** to contemplate. Brokerage companies invariably will consent to be taken over by another firm rather than cause the industry the humiliation and bad **investor publicity** associated with the trauma of bankruptcy.

When all is said and done, perhaps the best strategy for most investors would call for the investor to keep in his or her possession those stocks in which **complete control** is desired. All other stocks in which accumulation of income through dividends is perhaps the consideration for ownership, could be **relegated** to the custody of the **brokerage**.

SELECTING A STOCKBROKER:

A stockbroker, who is also known as an account executive or registered representative, is essentially a **salesperson** and not necessarily a good **stock picker**. He's qualified by virtue of having passed an examination that indicates he or she knows the required rules and laws which govern the buying and selling of securities with the general public. The brokers cannot obtain a broker's license on their own. They must generally be **sponsored** by a **brokerage firm** that normally has a trainee program in place. After an intensive training, they are permitted to take the test which upon passing enables them to secure their broker's license.

The broker is the industry's **contact** between you and the **great world** of securities investing. By establishing and preserving a good relationship with a broker, one is more apt to realize his or her maximum long term investment goals. The best thing a broker can provide for an investor is good research information, good service via order placements, and he should be readily available to correct problems that might arise in the clients account.

Good research is of course not generally available from a discount broker-age firm. The **discounter** generally acts more like a fast paced **order placement conduit** between the investor and whatever stock exchange is involved; and whereas no research is available, this translates to **lower commissions** than is required of the full service firms.

The decision of deciding between a full service broker or a discounter is an important one. The discounter will not help whatsoever when it comes to the client's stock picks, so the investor being on his or her own in the matter must do their research carefully to minimize errors which in this arena may very

well translate to dollar losses. Remember, that the discount broker runs a **bare-bones** operation that gives you no service, but will give you good execution on your trades, whereas the full-service broker will **recommend** stocks and **strategies** that he deems best for your situation. If you need guidance on some trades, but not on others, just remember that there's nothing unethical or immoral about dealing with **both types** of brokerage firms.

Before selecting a stock broker it's realistic that an investor determine what his or her investment needs and objectives are, and to what extent this investor might be primarily interested in a steady income, long term growth, quick profits, tax savings considerations; or possibly combination investments of one or more of these possibilities.

You may want to consult an **accountant** who understands your financial situation to help you outline the bounds of your financial objectives. Like — where do you want to be in ten years or twenty years from now?

People with **substantial assets** and **younger folks** generally find themselves able to take more **risks** for the potential larger profits down the road, as their long term investments grow through the appreciation and growth of their chosen securities. People in this catagory might also opt to invest some of their funds for intermediately quick profits resulting from flimsy-superficial and technical actions of certain stocks as they react in the market place.

On the other hand, those people who are **retired** and living on **fixed incomes** may be more attuned to securities that provide good regular income obtained from **dividends** and the shelter of secure **interest**. These people are highly motivated to protect their basic capital investment. If you're retired and along in years, you don't have the luxury of time to recoup on the heavy losses that might occur along the way, whereas a young person

IF YOU'RE
AN INVESTOR,
ACT LIKE ONE,
INVESTIGATE

having more years available would be better able to fight off substantial losses, and still retire "well fixed". Selecting the right broker should be done with the same care and attention as one would give to choosing any other professional such as a doctor or lawyer.

A good approach to this task is to ask for recommendations from the friends you know that are **successful** at investing. Ask other reliable people. This may be a business colleague, or your lawyer or accountant. Your **banker** could perhaps give you the names of good brokers; but keep in mind however, that someone else's broker may have particular strengths that are not necessarily good for your need or financial situation. The broker's **temperament** or investment **philosophy** may differ from yours.

When broker hunting, and you walk into a brokerage office looking for help, don't allow them to assign you to the "broker of the day". This would perhaps be a person on floor duty assigned to open new accounts and simply place your order. Maybe one of the best selection process is to meet with the office manager who will discuss your investment goals, and perhaps determine the type of investor he is dealing with. He will then try to **match you** with one of his brokers having particular knowledge in your area of interest.

Brokerage services are highly **private** and **personal**, so don't be miffed if your account executive asks you a few personal questions regarding your finances. Also, don't view his line of inquiry as an intrusion into your affairs. Your broker has a very **high sense** of discretion toward you the investor, and when it comes to divulging your business to an outsider, his candid make-up and keen sense of secretiveness would never allow him to damage your trust. (Those that kiss and tell don't last long.)

THE KEY TO STOCK VALUATION — EARNINGS

Your broker may ask questions concerning your net worth, the banks you deal with, your annual income, your cash-flow and liquidity needs. He'll want to know if you're investing for **short-term gains** or to build a **nest egg** for the future. He will also want to know your risk tolerance, investment objectives, you tax liability, and where you work. He may also have questions aimed at learning his client's investment experience. These questions constitute a **necessary dialogue** in many cases if the broker is to give the investor the maximum service that the investor is entitled to receive.

With all of the needed financial questions answered, both broker and client get to establish a **faith relationship** that rewards the client with good service, and that rewards the broker when all the elements of trust are present to make his job an easier one.

Having said all this, a word or two of caution is in order at this point. Investors ought to check carefully to see how much the broker pays attention to their accounts. Comparing notes with their friends to learn what their friends experience has been in this regard is a good idea.

If you're using a full-service broker, you're entitled to good service, research reports that come out periodically, buy and sell recommendations that you **don't** necessarily have to follow, and accurate monthly statements.

Investing is a **complex business**, and you'll be rewarded if you go into securities investing with your eyes "wide open". Try to realize that while your account executive is suppose to look after your interests, he is basically selling a product, and for his services he's allowed to pocket between 33% and 45% of the commissions you pay on every trade. His commission percentage often depends on how good he is at selling, and of course what

Time
is money.

brokerage firm has employed him. The full-service brokerage firms are constantly looking for brokers of the more **aggressive** "go-getter" variety whose consistant sales record prove that they can "get the order"—and close the deal.

If the broker is a young recruit who may only achieve a $75,000 to $100,000 commission for himself, chances are strong that he will receive but 25% of the commissions, or 25% of the $300,000 to $400,000 base commissions. This low commission schedule for the novice provides a strong incentive for him to improve his selling craft to the $200,000 commission level for himself, where he may receive 33% to 37% of commissions plus other perks.

The really big producers — brokers generating about $1,000,000 of commissions might be on a 45% commission schedule. This would guarantee the broker $450,000 of commission salary. He would then possibly be entitled to a $100,000 bonus, that would effectively give him or her in excess of 50% of the generated commissions. We're talking now about the "big boys" or the "big girls" as the case might be, those generating big commissions because they have solid contacts with the people having big money for investments.

The people dealing with the "top shelf" brokers place a good deal of confidence in these brokers based generally on their **superior track record** of making money for their clients. These brokers are well known in the brokerage business, and they will be wined and dined, and courted lavishly just as the prized football players would be for their services to the NFL football owners. These brokers are so good at what they do that brokerage people having designs on one of these sales persons might very well hand this broker a six figure bonus "up front" to wean them over from their competitive firm — knowing full well of course that when a broker of that

KEEP ON
TOP OF THE
ACTIVITY IN
YOUR ACCOUNT

caliber leaves his firm the **clients go** with that **broker**.

When choosing a broker you may rest assured that the chances are slim to none that if you're a small or medium investor, the high powered broker is not for you. He's so busy with his millionaire clients that his schedule does not allow for servicing small to medium accounts. These star brokers are shielded from the general public by their brokerage firm, and the only way you could possibly meet one would be in his service elevator.

The broker is required by the various stock exchanges to use "due diligence" in servicing the customer's accounts. He can only discharge diligence if he **really knows** his customer. The customer-investor should continually update his situation with the broker if there is any important change in his financial situation or investment goals.

When a broker recommends a security to a client, he or she should do so on the basis of **good reasoning**, and not on some **premonition** or **hunch.** There is nothing wrong with asking your broker to provide you with the **research materials** that he used as the groundwork for recommending a certain security.

Good brokers will consider a client's needs vis-a-vis the security that he or she is recommending. They will also take into account the investor's **degree** of **sophistication**, his knowledge of the business, and his investment objectives.

Investors should understand that one's professional acumen in his or her own chosen field of endeavor does not automatically translate to being a successful investor. This is why, generally speaking, the average investor should make the trading decisions in **consultation** with the broker. Unbeknown to the investor, the broker could very likely have a bit of current information that would **preclude trading** at a particular time.

BROKER RECOMMATIONS:

When a broker suggests a specific stock selection for a client, it may not be based on the broker's own judgment. The individual account executive might have preferred to give the client a different selection. At many of the large brokerage firms the **research departments** dictate the **approved list** of stocks from which their brokers may pick and choose as investment ideas for their investor clients.

Any stocks that are not on the approved list will generally be treated as off-limits. This is **arbitrary marketing** and may of course work to the detriment of the investor; but this is not to say that an investor may not purchase any stock of his or her choice. This forcing of stocks may perhaps happen more frequently when **research departments** get too **powerful**, and they seem to want control of all the transactions.

When a **compliance department** is stronger in the corporate framework of a brokerage than the research arm of marketing, this recommended list becomes a weaker factor to the individual broker, and he's then allowed to use some of his own ideas in making suggestions to his clients.

Since the brokerage people that set up strong research departments insist that their suggested lists be implimented by their brokers, it's perhaps unfair to fault them, because sizeable amounts of money goes into this research. Some brokers feel a definite restriction when using only the research recommended stocks. However, some also feel that it gets the onus off their back so far as the brokerage is concerned, if the suggestion goes sour on the investor.

When a broker makes a suggestion to a client outside his firm's recommended list, he needs only to have a **reasonable basis** for his recommendations, backed perhaps by his own file on the particular stock.

Some account executives become highly adept at pushing packaged products such as mutual funds and tax shelters which return a bigger "buck" than the regular stock commissions. Just suppose that you're an account executive with a designated menu of products for sale. You now see that you may sell a limited partnership for ten times the income you would derive from a listed bond or stock. "Ten to one" you would try selling the partnership.

The name of the game at the brokerage house is sales. Therefore, any research list has to be"tailored" in such a way that it will be **bought** by the investor. The list cannot be made up of "antique" untimely suggestions, or it won't go over with the investors who will turn negative on the shabby, time decayed ideas.

Brokerage firms like to think that their registered representatives will be viewed by the general public as well-qualified investment advisers rather than the high-pressure stock and bond sales people that they have come to represent. However, as investors, let's not be dismayed — nothing is **perfect**, and there is a definite necessity of producing income for the company and its reps. This necessity is what pushes new reps into using "fast buck" sales techniques normally employed in less flattering fields.

Still, long term, a broker's livelyhood depends on his developing and maintaining long-term relationships with his customers. This is a **turnover business** where the clients will only return if they are treated **properly**.

to err is human and costly

DEALING WITH BROKER'S ERRORS:

While brokers' errors may be an aggravation, we should try to remember that our broker may be handling many transactions, and he may not always be the one at fault. The back-office help that handle the paper work are accurate people, but things can go wrong, and this is especially true during periods of heavy trading volume. Example — The obscene stock market disaster of October 19th 1987, when the Dow Industrials **lost 508 points** in the worst stock market debacle in history.

**DON'T WORRY IF YOU'VE MISSED
THE CHANCE OF A LIFETIME
GET ON TO NEW BUSINESS**

Your **obligation** of course is to be sure that your broker understands your order **completely.** Your broker should repeat your order back to you, thereby ensuring that there's been no breakdown in communication. All good brokers will call you to **verify** the execution of your order. Pay close attention when he or she does, because some brokers, especially of the discount variety, will talk fast, and slam the horn down quickly to get on to his other calls (or new business). An important buy or sell order from you becomes a routine matter-of-fact transaction to him. Also, you will come to realize that while you may be at your leisure sipping a nice cool drink while placing your order, he on the other hand is busy **fighting the clock** to get his share of orders as time fleets-away.

When placing an order with your broker, write it out completely and read it from your notes to the broker. This provides you with **documentation** with which to compare when the broker **calls back** to confirm, and which also can be viewed against the **confirmation slip** when it arrives in the mail.

Never be **hesitant** about asking questions of your broker, and don't be afraid to **disagree** with his suggested recommendation. Your broker deals continuously in yes or no factors, so don't fear **saying no**, for fear of offending him — these people are not thin skinned. Work closely with your broker, and if there is anything you don't understand, call him at once—**don't walt.**

Some of the errors that may occur at the brokerage involve buying the wrong number of shares,splitting the order, thus generating more commissions for the broker. Getting into the wrong company name, or charging the transaction to the wrong account where dual accounts are held by the investor, are

42

other examples of possible errors that might occur. The order might be incorrectly placed — that is, market order, versus limit, versus stop loss order.

The broker might have erred in marking the sale as a day order, a weekly order, or an open order which is generally in force for a month before requiring renewal. The order could conceivably have been placed at the wrong price. The wrong broker commission might have been applied to the transaction — a likely back-office error.

Always keep in mind that a brokerage firm is liable for the **consequences** of its errors, when such errors affect a customer. So, if your broker **goofs** and it costs you **excessive dollars**, demand that the difference be made up to you. Your broker is primarily in **sales** and not in the **restitution** business; so if he **goofs**, you must call it to his attention and firmly follow through (if necessary with the manager). You naturally have no recourse if your stocks simply lose value based on market declines — here you're on your own.

However! if you should own a stock currently selling, shall we say at $31.00 a share, and you have a good-till-cancel stop loss order to sell the stock at $28.00 and the stock goes lower than $28.00 and you're not sold out; your broker in all **probability** has made a serious **error of execution**, and you can demand that the difference be made up to you.

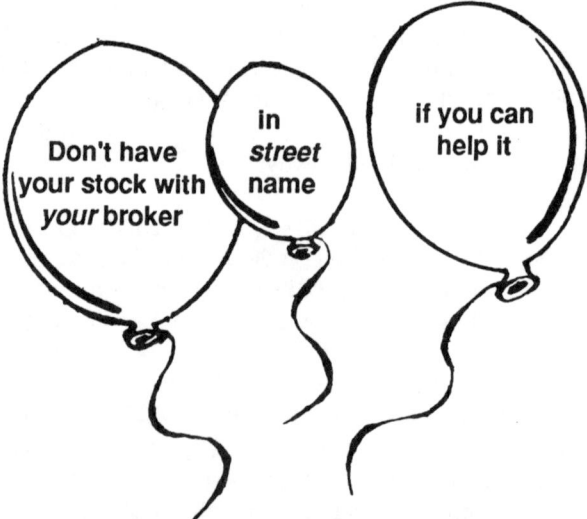

All customer complaints at your brokerage must be heeded by management per a ruling of the securities industry **self-regulatory** units. These self-regulations emanate primarily from the New York Stock Exchange or the

National Association of Securities Dealers, and are induced by the "Watch dog" of the industry—**The Securities** and **Exchange Commission**. When a discrepancy or disagreement arises one should first talk to the broker. He may be unaware of operational **snafus,** (Situations normal all fouled-up) but with the help of his customer service department he may be able to clear up the problem. Gather together the required supporting documents to substantiate your claim, such as the order and confirm slips, along with relevant monthly statements. If these have to be mailed, don't part with your originals, mail photocopies.

Failing satisfaction with the broker one should talk to the branch manager who holds a heavy responsibility to see that the investor is not mistreated, and to make sure that a complaint is not ignored or mishandled in any way. The branch manager has good **latitude powers** to settle disputes. However, in large or important settlements the investor might be wise to have an **attorney review** the pre-arbitration settlement to assure that the investor is being given a "fair shake". Some 30% of the problems that arise which are handled initially at the branch manager's level are said to be resolved satisfactorily for the investor.

Investors must not lose sight of the fact that brokers make commissions **every time** they execute whether it is on the buy or sell side of a transaction, or whether an investor makes money or loses money on a transaction.

BROKERS AND ARBITRATION:

Don't get caught behind the 8 ball.

When an investor and a brokerage house reach an **impasse** whereby a dispute regarding transactions cannot be resolved to the agreement of an investor, the investor-client may go to **arbitration**. This means that the investor may submit his case to an arbitration panel of three to five arbitrators who after considering the evidence on both sides of the dispute will render a **binding judgment** against either the brokerage company or the investor.

The U.S. Supreme Court ruled on June 8th of 1987 that except in very few instances all securities disputes between brokers and investor clients would **henceforth** be resolved by the arbitration panels of the Securities Industry Conference on Arbitration (SICA), **if** the **signed documentations** between the broker and client called for arbitration of disputes.

Most brokerage firms have the arbitration clause as part of their brokerage agreement; so, in the future it would seem that the vast majority of serious disputes would necessarily go to arbitration. By this decision the high court has ruled out court action as a viable alternative to arbitration. Investors had developed the habit of **disregarding** the pre-dispute arbitration clauses of their broker applications, and were **actively suing** in the courts rather than submitting their disputes to arbitration prior to the June 1987 Supreme Court decision.

The rising sales volume in the brokerage business in recent years has opened a "flood gate" of customer complaints concerning some of the **abusive practices** employed by stockbrokers. The complaints against brokers that were documented by the Securities and Exchange Commission during 1982 totaled close to 6900 as compared to an escalated figure of 16,000 in 1986. Also, the number of **securities-related** arbitration cases increased by a factor of more than three, from about 800 in 1980 to some 2800 cases in 1985.

Think About It.

The Supreme Court was perhaps highly motivated to remove the aggrieved investor's recourse to the courts by the ever increasing case load that found its way into the judicial system. Some people representing **investor group's interests** don't particularly relish the idea of what is now effectively **forced arbitration** with **no appeal** proceedures, and possible loss of chances for **punitive damages**.

Normally, there would be more than enough professional savvy in the arbitration arena to render sound decisions, thereby relieving the courts of this **highly specialized** work. However, with the implimentation of the court decision, the job of arbitration has suddenly become a larger and more important one in scope, and this is especially so since the stock market's debacle of October 1987, when the Dow Jones Industrial average lost over 1000 points in short order — not to mention the Supreme Court decision of June 1987 which had the immediate effect of driving potential court cases directly to the arbitration hearings.

Sensing this **crushing load** of arbitration cases being foisted upon the current arbitration system by the June of 1987 high court decision, the Securities and Exchange Commission recommended extensive **rule changes** designed to improve the fairness and efficiency of the securities industry arbitration system for the settling of broker versus customer disputes. The Commissioners unanimously adopted a set of changes in the industry's **arbitration code** that would lessen the potential for conflicts of interest and improve the public's confidence in arbitration as a sound way of settling investor disputes. S.E.C. Chairman David Ruder believes that customers must be treated **more fairly**, and that customers must actually believe that they are being treated fairly. This is not an easy job when the opposing self interests of both the investor and broker is at issue.

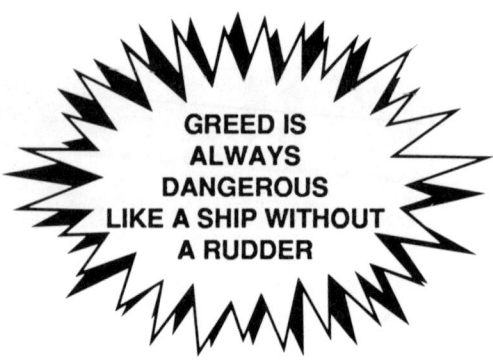

**GREED IS
ALWAYS
DANGEROUS
LIKE A SHIP WITHOUT
A RUDDER**

The S.E.C. actions will **shore up** the arbitration proceedures and are expected to quicken good will acceptance toward arbitration as an alternative to the litigation of disputes. Arbitrators are generally selected from 2 rosters: a panel of 3 consisting of one panalist-arbitrator from the securities industry list, and two panalists representing the general public, from the general public roster.

Here-to-fore the industry tended to "fudge" by possibly assigning a general public panalist who had a **natural bias** toward the **industry** — such as retired employees, or **lawyers** who had a past history of representing the industry on arbitration panels. Can't you just see a beautifully "stacked deck" **against** the **investor** at the panel hearings! The S.E.C. now recommends barring those with significant **professional ties** to the securities industry from participating on the **public arbitrator** roster.

Those professionals who had been assigned in the past to the public roster would be transferred to the **industry roster** of arbitrators. Even spouses of industry employees could no longer serve under the proposed new rules as public arbitrators. This would transfer 600 to perhaps 800 people from the public to the industry roster.

Among other things the S.E.C. is recommending that the securities industry set up education programs for **developing good arbitrators**, and that a training manual be developed along these lines. The S.E.C. further suggests that industry improve its methods of **evaluating** the **credentials** of prospective arbitrators. Also, the S.E.C. is recommending that more disclosure be instituted, enabling those involved in the web of an arbitration proceeding to have a good idea of the personal, social, and business interests of those on the panel vis-a-vis their interests; thereby reducing the possibility of discrimanations and conflicts of interests. Under the new rules, (SICA) The Securities Industry Conference on Arbitration would be required to obtain a ten year **business biography** on all active arbitrators, and that these

Think Again.

biographies would be available to the parties in arbitration who have a right to reject two arbitrators **for cause**, and one arbitrator **without cause**.

The new suggested rules would allow depositions from witnesses, and allow enough time for all involved to produce the necessary documentation to support their positions. Punitive damages against the industry will perhaps be highly contested by the industry. However, investors might like to contend that this is a trade off — of investors now losing a right to trial by jury, not to mention the **loss** of the **appeal process**.

The Securities Industry Conference on Arbitration is the body that sets up the **rules** which are followed by the **panel arbitrators**, and this conference in cooperation with the National Association of Securities Dealers, the New York Stock Exchange, and other arbitration sponsors (exchanges) will finalize the new set of **rules** that will govern arbitration in the future — barring any intervening legislation from the federal people.

Securities arbitration is normally handled like a court case. Both sides present their evidence and while there is no requirement that an investor be represented by counsel, he or she had better have an attorney along; because it's a safe bet that the brokers will be well represented by lawyers that are **highly skilled** in **securities** law.

The advantage of arbitration lies in the fact that it's **less expensive** to pursue, is **faster**, and is **less formal** than litigation in courts. The "track record" seems to be that in about 50% of arbitration cases the award has gone to the client. Therefore, it would seem reasonable to believe that with the addition of more arbitration panels and the upcoming improvements being pushed by the S.E.C., the 50% figure favoring investors could be improved.

Securities lawyers are a special breed. He alone can help you in arbitration or litigation matters.

Despite the above comments, the **final** rules **may yet** be **dictated** by the **legislative** process. People representing investors are not very happy with the pre-dispute arbitration clauses in place at most brokerage houses in which an estimated 90% of retail customers have no choice; but are subjected to the pre-dispute arbitration provisions which is part of the stock account documentation. The idea of loss of the **judicial process**, and right to trial by judge or jury in which the appeal process is alive, and not dependent in any way by the industry, is of course **precious** to the people representing investor groups.

While the institutions have the **money clout** to **negotiate away** the pre-dispute arbitration clauses, the regular retail customers don't; unless an individual customer comes along with the really **big bucks**. This power by some to **overcome** the signing of the arbitration clause puts Mr. Average Investor over a "barrel". The net effect is **discriminatory** to a vast majority of investors; as the forced arbitration system **denies** people access to the securities industry, **unless** they sign such an application clause.

At this writing it looks as though the House Energy and Commerce Committee, the Securities and Exchange Commission, and some members of Congress are pushing toward elimination of the **mandatory aspect** of the pre-dispute arbitration clauses, thus getting the entire securities investment industry **rid** of this **absence** of **choice** in settling disputes, which many investors think will settle some **fundamental** questions concerning investor protection. The final legislative curbs might even allow the industry to give special perks such as **lower commission rates** for those investors who might be agreeable to going along with the pre-dispute arbitration clause.

Securities industry people would not be hesitant to say that arbitration is a fair and effective way of handling disputes, and they may very well be right; but I would suspect that the upcoming legislative regulations will take the

forced feature out of the pre-dispute arbitration clauses in effect at most brokerage houses.

The Securities and Exchange Commission also wants a **speed-up** of the **process** to resolve disputes in faster more equitable ways. One way would involve calling for a $10,000 ceiling on small claims instead of the current $5,000 ceiling. Also, utilizing but one arbitrator in such small claims instead of the current three that preside. Presently many claims up to the $5,000 level are simply settled amicably by a written claim letter to the broker.

The brokerage people will make **serious efforts** to settle all claims of an **indisputable nature** against them before such claims go to arbitration. Meantime, so many errors are supposedly being made by this **fast-buck mania** of the last five year bull market, which culminated in the market calamity of Black Monday and Tuesday of Oct. 19-20 1987; that it's understandable that these errors are generating claims that place tremendous pressures on an arbitration system that is scrambling desperately to expand its **arbitrator panels** in efforts to meet its increased responsibilities to the general investing public.

The Massachusetts security regulators, in a move designed to help investors, passed a regulation scheduled to become effective Jan.1,1989, and designed to **eliminate mandatory arbitration** of disputes that occur between brokers and investors. The new regulation mandates that brokers advise investors of their constitutional right to take their **disputes to court.** The Massachusetts regulation which is expected to be duplicated soon in a dozen of other states, also specifies that brokers cannot refuse to do business with an investor who refuses to **sign** the **pre-dispute arbitration statement** that calls for mandatory arbitration.

The Massachusetts regulators don't have a "beef" with the arbitration process, but they want consumers to have a choice. The regulators have a good size laundry list of **complaints relative** to **mandatory arbitration.** They especially don't believe that the less **risky cash customers** should be forced into an arbitration agreement.

Meanwhile, the Securities Industry Association whose representatives testified at public hearings against the Massachusetts regulation in July of 1988, are preparing to **challenge** this regulation in court on constitutional grounds. It also appears that the Securities Industry Association will try to prove that the Supreme Court decision of June 1987 relative to arbitration proceedures takes presidence, and **somehow nullifies** the Massachusetts regulation.

It's interesting to contemplate that for a number of years everyone seemed to be making money in the market, and no one seemed to be upset over the signing of the pre-dispute arbitration applications. However, it took the 15,000 calls to the Security Administrator's Association **post-crash hotline**, to reveal that most of these hotline complaints were about the **unfairness** of **forced arbitration.**

GUARD AGAINST

HIGH-PRESSURE

SALES PITCHES

CHURNING:

Churning is an abuse of **authority** by a broker, characterized by **excessive** trading of a customer's account that results in an abnormally large commission "take" for the broker, and may produce heavy losses for the investor. Churning generally takes place in a **discretionary account** in which the trader-investor has signed a **stock power** that effectively gives the broker **unlimited** authority to trade in that customer's account. A discretionary account might be okay for a **busy professional** who doesn't have time to devote to his own trading decisions; but only if the investor has had a **long standing** securities client-broker relationship. Otherwise, the discretionary account is for the "fillu-lulu" birds. There is too much availability temptation for the broker who is given discretionary power to abuse the account by **over-trading**. This is especially the case in the large brokerage firms that often put great pressures on their brokers to generate commissions via the Monday morning **staff meeting**; where too often the "bugaboos" of pride, envy, greed, and avarice dominate as the motivational **qualities** of the day — not normally expected from a group of so-called high class professionals.

Investor groups generally put out the **caution light** against **discretionary** accounts in which the broker calls all the "shots" making all the buy and sell decisions in a customer's account.

The industry has done an outstanding job of **policing itself** over the years, but in an industry where a fantastic amount of money is involved, temptation becomes great for the **unscrupulous.**

BEWARE OF RUMORS AND TIPS OF BIG PROFITS

Policing of brokerage office operations is done by **compliance officers** who concentrate on uncovering abuses of public confidence. These abuses include domination over the unsophisticated investor, using **high-pressure** sales tactics — especially those aimed toward the weak, the elderly, and the widows. The policing of brokers further consists of looking for **misrepresentations** in the form of strong statements such as — "how can you miss" or "the stock will surely go up". They look into the margin operations, and they scrutinize the weak accounts where there is clearly a **lack of capitalization** with which to cope with the **risks** involved. The policing people also look for **reckless incompetence** of brokers who tout highly speculative stocks (cats & dogs) for **retired investors** to whom safety of their basic capital is of utmost importance to them.

Additionally, they try to uncover situations in which a brokerage does not disclose an interest in a security that the brokerage might be promoting vigorously to enhance the value of its own holding to the obvious detriment of the investors.

The key elements a compliance officer seems to be looking for are lack of **honesty and fairness** toward the investor. The motivation for the exchanges to police their operations has come repeatedly over the years from the Securities and Exchange Commission. The S.E.C. promises to "come down hard" on the **stock markets** if they don't keep their "houses" squeaky clean.

The unfortunate practice on the part of a small percentage of brokers to be instrumental in customers buying and selling securities more often than they should, can generate excessive commission costs for customers, and may be counter productive vis-a-vis the customer's best interests. This "churning" practice when taken to **an extreme** may very well result in severe penalties to the broker, and to his brokerage firm if it is **encouraging** him in this practice.

The contested cases of abuse that go to arbitration normally have to do with **complaints** such as:

> Unauthorized trades.
> Trades executed in an inappropriate manner.
> Failure to deliver the securities to the investor.
> Churning the account — known as excessive trading.
> Lying, exagerating or just plain BSing (bum steering),
>   which amounts to misrepresenting the facts.
> Unsuitable investments — generally attributed to brokers
>   who give high-risk investment advice for low-risk investors.

Suitability has to do with the investor's objectives, their ages, their known degree of financial sophistication, and the investors remaining assets.

We know that a broker is not a God, nor does he have **clairvoyant abilities**; so, his buy recommendations often amount to a **crapshoot** in which an investor is the **unwary participant**.

If the broker's suggested stock rises, the investor will naturally be happy and the broker will stay in touch with the investor, realizing that he has increased the possibility of doing more trades for this customer. In the unfortunate event that a suggested stock drops, there is no incentive for some brokers to contact the investor. Even if he called the client to suggest that the client sell to cut his losses short, he'll perhaps still get himself a hard time from his customer for **recommending** a **losing stock**.

This reminds me of the story concerning lawyers. They're never **quite heroes** with most people, because even though they may have worked like "dogs" and won their case, the **appreciation** and **gratitude** factor by most clients is "short circuited" by the fact that now, this **big fee** has to be **paid**. Oh well! so much for gratitude. Good brokers keep in touch with clients, because next to **buying right**, cutting one's **losses short** is what investing is all about.

BEWARE!
Has a broker corralled you into getting
discretionary power over your account?

Some stockbrokers occasionally fail to understand and act upon the fact that, even though a customer does not vest formal discretionary authority with them; they none the less exercise **"control"** over that account if the customer is relatively naive and unsophisticated in the realm of **market operations**, and relies **solely** on the broker's expertise.

A degree of control sufficient to warrant **protection** would perhaps be in place if the investor's facts clearly established that this customer **invariably relied** on the dealer's recommendations. The volume and frequency of transactions suggested by a broker would of course be a **crucial element** in finding that **churning** occurred on the part of the broker.

Transactions involving **multiple trading** in the same security, and many **switches** from security to security are taboo in the industry; and where excessive commissions are generated while disregarding the customer's **investment objectives** is considered to be fraudulent trading within the meaning of the Federal securities acts.

Compliance Officer

ANATOMY OF A SECURITY COMPLIANCE OFFICER:

Despite what has been done in the past by the compliance department of securities firms to prevent wrongdoings by their employees and clients, there remains much work to be done. The rash of scandals that have occurred in recent years has prompted the S.E.C. to suggest that brokerage firms spend **more dollars** on their **compliance** departments. The congressional investigators have concurred in this.

One of the large Wall Street firms was fined over 25 million dollars in 1987 by the Fed. for failing to uncover **insider trading** and other securities law violations that were currently prevalent within the firm. It's the compliance officer's **duty** to help prevent such **violations** within the firm. The Securities and Exchange Commission and the exchanges themselves have been placing **more pressure** on the securities firms to spot the **lawbreakers**. This translates to more pressure on the compliance departments that seem to be grossly **understaffed**.

Compliance officers seem to believe that insider trading is one of the most difficult violations to spot. They grouse that very often they have neither the information, nor the **investigative authority** to uncover such a wrongdoing. They furthur complain of the many potential sources of information available to would be violators, and of the many ways that violators employ to **cover-up** their illegal activities. Some of the experts in this area of activity believe that if an individual inside violator is willing to take the proper precautions to conceal his or her activities, it becomes **nearly impossible** to detect such an individual.

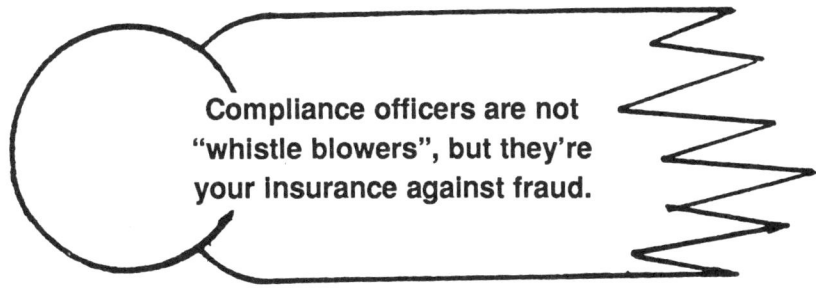

Compliance officers are not "whistle blowers", but they're your insurance against fraud.

Compliance officers are occasionally viewed by some of the personnel within a security firm as being "whistle blowers". This isn't surprising if we consider the very **bare-bones staff** they have in relation to the size of their entire organization. One of the large prestigious Wall Street firms that employs 5000 people has a tiny officer compliance department of only 10 **people**. Another firm, that is just about the largest in the business, and that employs roughly 43,000 people, has a compliance department of **merely 100 people**. We're talking now about an industry that is very structured, tight knit, and very discrete with its affairs.

While the position of compliance officer is a very important one as perceived by investors "looking up" to this industry for fair play, the job has not in the past received the **cooperation** and **attention** that it deserves in the securities industry **corporate** structure. While the compliance officer slot generally requires intelligence and good investigative skills, the pay is not that great. While most firms may not have too much trouble filling the senior investigators slots, they have their problems **hiring the workhorses**; those talented employees capable of scanning the many computer printouts that are generated by the electronic surveillance systems. With a pay scale of roughly $25,000 per year for junior officers just out of college, one has to think seriously about the potential "pecking order" **damage** that can very easily be contrived against these **junior compliance** people.

The potential advancement clout that may be applied against a $25,000 a year compliance officer trying to police employees, some of which earn several **million dollars** a year, can certainly be devastating career-wise, and especially if the young compliance officer has uncovered a "big fish"—an important bigwig caught **red-handed** in a big insider trading deal. It's that **big money** that wields great power when a VIP is caught in the "cookie jar" of insider trading.

Compliance officers contend that it's those inventive and **creative inside traders** that are the most troublesome to apprehend and "put away". These insider traders use pay phones liberally. They also trade in several accounts, and firm name accounts, spreading these accounts liberally among several countries.

Nevertheless, most of the securities firms would not hesitate in saying that the industry does a **reasonably good job** of nabbing those whose misdeeds they uncover within their ranks, and of reporting to the S.E.C. those insider violations which emanate from clients, or investors outside of their offices.

When investors buy their initial stock deal, they are very apt to buy because of what someone they knew might have told them. If one gets involved listening to other people such as friends concerning the buying of securities, one should be assured that such a person has done **adequate research.** Most people, though meaning well, and purporting to have inside information, seldom do, and this may be costly to the **naive listener** who hopes to get that hot tip which usually has already been **discounted** at the market place.

**NEVER BUY A STOCK
YOU CAN'T WATCH**

MARGIN ACCOUNTS:

The margin account is the speculator's **number one tool**. This is buying on credit. If the speculator understands the account and is good at using it, there are handsome profits that may be made. If he or she plays this game poorly, the losses may be disastrous — like playing blackjack "Vegas style".

The margin account application that an investor signs hypothecates the account, thus **pledging** the **securities** in the account to the use of the broker. This account is unlike the usual cash account in which the securities are held by the broker at the investor's option, but merely for safekeeping purposes.

When you buy stock on margin, the broker puts up half the money, and **effectively becomes your partner**. In exchange for this service, the broker requires that you give him this permission to use **your securities.** This seems like a good enough deal, for after all, financially it's half his anyway — having put up half the cost of the transaction. The investor who uses a margin account is still entitled to the dividends, and to the **decision making process** concerning the account, providing the investor maintains the proper margin requirement on transactions.

If you should want to buy stocks but don't want to invest the full value, a margin account allows you currently to put up 50% of the purchase price, and to borrow the remainder from your stock broker. Margin buying is a **quick** and comparatively easy way to **borrow money**. Margin allows you to use your **dormant assets** (stocks) at your broker without moving or selling them. However, it's by no stretch of the imagination a **safe bet**. Gains and losses are magnified and the typical buyer would be someone who's traded for a number of years, and **knows his way around** in dealing with brokers.

NEVER OVER-EXTEND YOURSELF.

He is especially knowledgeable in that big word—**risk**.

Let's say you have $10,000 in cash or marginable securities, and you've become aware of a good buy in the market, but you need $20,000. Your margined $10,000 will enable you to buy this $20,000 deal. If the $20,000 stock deal doubles to $40,000, your profit is $20,000 less interest on the $10,000 that the broker borrows from the bank to accomodate your deal. If the stock lost 50% of its value, you would lose your entire $10,000 plus interest, but the brokers would not lose their $10,000.

When your **broker borrows money** at his bank and lends it to you, enabling you to buy stocks on margin, he has to provide the bank with some **security** for the loan. This security may very likely be the stock that you are buying through your margin account. This is the **exact reason** why assets in a margin account have to be hypothecated, or pledged to the use of the broker.

When a stock declines **beyond** the point secured by the assets in the margin account, which currently is a 50% asset posture, the broker has to send the investor a **margin call** requiring the investor to "come up" with more money to again bring the account up to the **regulation** 50% required for all margin accounts.

Failure on the part of the investor to answer the margin call will automatically force the broker to sell enough of the stock to maintain the account at the correct percentage required by the margin maintenance rules. If the broker-age sees a **downtrend** in the margined stock, the broker may call for **more margin** than is immediately necessary, in anticipation of further declines in that margined stock, thus avoiding the need to call again soon after the original call.

Most margin customers actually maintain margin positions in several stocks. In this situation the margin call from the broker will refer to the margin position of the **entire account** and not the margin status of one stock that may have fallen below the maintenance level established by the brokerage firm. Here's where the modern **data processing** and **computer equipment** at brokers comes into play. By balancing surpluses and shortages, these machines come up **instantly** with a customer's overall **debit/credit position.**

Buyers of securities on margin have an **extensive list** of "goodies" available to them. They may use their margin account to buy virtually all stocks that are trading in excess of $3.00 per share on the major exchanges, or in the over-the-counter market. This is also the account used when the investor wants to **sell short.** Certain over-the-counter stocks that are sparsely traded and highly volatile are on a list of stocks that **don't qualify** for buying on margin.

Most brokers seem to recommend that investors confine their margin activity to the stocks of the big, strong, and stable companies — those shares that trade well, having great amounts of **stock outstanding** with the general public.

Investors buying on margin should know what margin is all about. They should know what their broker's maintenance rules are, because **maintaning enough equity** in their account to satisfy both the broker and government regulations could be the investor's greatest problem.

DON'T TAKE
ADVICE
FROM THE
UNINFORMED.

SELLING SHORT:

Investors who sell short are adopting a **betting stance** that the market prices will fall. To sell short, the investor borrows shares from someone who owns them. This borrowed stock could come from the **broker's inventory** of that stock, or, it most likely will come from stock that is held in various customer's **margin accounts.**

The margin investor who anticipates that the price of a stock will decline may sell short the stock, and if it declines, he's able to "cover" by buying long the same shares at a lower price, thus returning the shares to the lending investor. The investor who shorted will **pocket** the **difference** between the two transactions if the borrowed stock actually goes down in price. In this illustration if the borrowed stock goes up in price, the investor that shorted would suffer a **loss** if he covered his borrowed transaction while the borrowed stock was higher in price than when it was borrowed. All these transactions are done **very quickly** — perhaps in a matter of minutes or even seconds by the **brokers** when the customer's account is in order.

Some people who don't understand the margin account, and the shorting privilege that goes with it, tend to believe that selling short is somehow **gambling**. However, selling a stock short and hoping that the stock will decrease in value, is no more a gamble than buying a stock long and **praying** to your favorite diety that it will go up in price. Despite all the logical explanations that may be offered to justify short selling, the practice still conjures up **horrors** in the minds of **some folks**.

If we think that it's O.K. to buy stocks because we think that they will go up in price, why isn't it O.K. to make a profit when they go down? Why should we not be able to make profits in either direction? In actuality the right of the bear to go short is just as essential to a completely **free market** as the right of a bull to go long (buying stocks outright). In fact, shorting injects more **liquidity** into the market and this tends to bring prices into closer "sync" with real values.

For many professional investors, the shorting of stocks is **standard procedure**, and this strategy is used more readily in flat/bearish markets where selective buying and shorting is used to attain profits from the few stocks, the prices of which may be on the move.

Most brokers would perhaps say that there is no good reason why **knowledgeable** investors should not use short selling as part of an **all inclusive** investment strategy.

Who lends all these shares that investors use to sell short? They are other investors who are typically in the same game; those having **margin accounts** at their brokerage firms, and who buy stock on margin from their brokerages.

**Short selling
is
expressing
your judgment
of
future events**

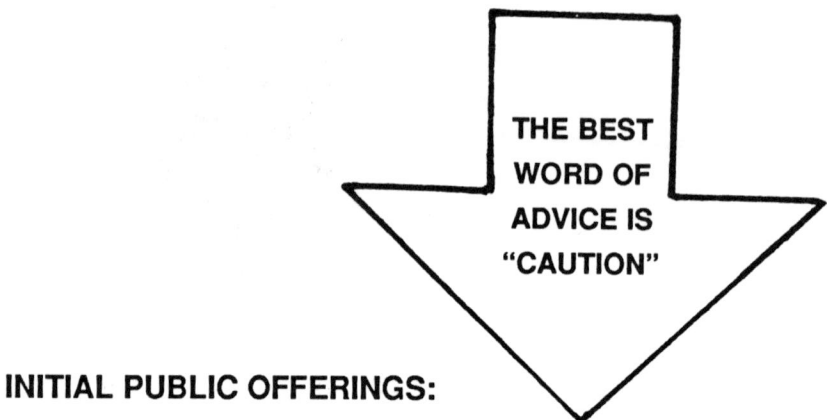

THE BEST
WORD OF
ADVICE IS
"CAUTION"

INITIAL PUBLIC OFFERINGS:

We're talking now about **new companies**, and perhaps their main source of financing to start up, and to operate on a continuous basis. Enter the investment bankers who, for a commission, will float some stocks or bonds onto the market to raise funds for a specified group of entrepreneurs — thus enabling the group to start its business. The managing investment bankers, also known as underwriters, form a **syndicate** with the **brokerage houses** that are willing to go in on the primary distribution. These underwriters are the people who advertise the offerings and **put them over**.

The initial public offerings do not have to be sold onto a stock exchange, but if the new company does not go public (onto an exchange), the new shares are sold **privately** or through the dealers of the **over-the-counter market.**

While the profits from initial public offerings may be good for an investor, the risks are much greater than those of the well established companies having good market histories. If one must take the plunge into IPOs, a **basic-industry-group** company might return some very good profits to investors having a **low risk** tolerance, whereas those faddy, new idea, high-tech whisper issues could, and very often do, spell out unhealthy losses for the participants.

Some of these initial public offerings are hot, and some are not. The temptation is great at times to get involved with IPOs as hundreds of them come out every year. These constitute a product line that your broker has **comitted** to **sell you** when his brokerage joins the syndicate that is set up by the underwriters (bankers); so, don't be surprised if the next call you get from your account executive is one suggesting that you get in on the ground floor of this hot "dud" he may be peddling.

**MORE SPECULATORS
LOSE MONEY
THAN MAKE MONEY**

If his hot issue isn't part of your risk reward strategy, "**just say no**", like a real cynic — but keep your cash intact.

During bull market times such as those we experienced during the five years prior to the market disaster of Oct. 19, 1987, the primary offerings were popular and quite successful in their start-ups because **money was flush**. This was a time of euphoria when market place psychology seemed to be saying that everything would succeed. This was also an advantageous time for underwriters who underwrote issues for many hundreds of small new companies in any given year.

During **bear market eras** the underwriters will "cool their heels", and not be so anxious to underwrite for companies the stock of which will not be so readily snatched-up by the investors at the brokerage level.

Before buying into an IPO, investors should be asking a number of questions:— are present market conditions O.K. for this issue? Is the price right? Is this hot issue in a solid industry group? If the new company has a history, what is it? What use will be made of the raised money? What is the quality of the new company's management? Are the underwriters from a reputable firm?

This initial public offering arena is one that is generally **froth with speculation** and should ordinarily be avoided by the small and medium type investors. However, if you wish to play the IPO "sweepstakes", ask your broker to supply you with advance notice of new issues he handles. This will enable your broker to mail **indications** of **interest** to you which are **non-binding orders** on both customers and brokers. These orders to buy an IPO in advance of the sale and before the price is set, will help to determine the **buying interest** at the retail level. The placing of the actual buy order comes later.

The initial advertising effort on an IPO comes several weeks before the stock offering when money managers and **big wig investors** are invited to **sales pitches** presented by the underwriters and the new company executives. These **presentations** will give institutional money managers the opportunity to size up the **caliber** of management vis-a-vis the **new company plans**, and best of all, will enable the money managers to guage and measure each others interest in the new offering.

Whereas a new company has no history of past performance with which to compare, it's a good idea to compare what will be an **existing competitor's company** with the **prospectus** and other information available from the new company. These **comparables** can be of help to evaluate a new company.

The quality and size of an underwriting firm may make a blg difference in the success or failure of an I.P.O. distribution, and its success on the open market for the first year. The chances are strong that the larger underwriting firm may have a **stronger** distribution capacity that enables it to stimulate more excitement about the offering. From an investor's point of view it's important to know how the distribution is going as the **trading date** approaches on the open market.

The smart investors get bad "vibes" if the offering is only **partially sold** on market opening day. With this scenario the stock will lack **public demand** to push the stock upward, as the underwriter's group struggles to complete the distribution.

When the offering has been **fully committed** to on trading day, the stock has a better chance of appreciating on the first few days of trading. The investor seems to have a better situation if the offering is **over-subscribed** when the

NEVER BUY
ON THE
BASIS OF
RUMORS OR
SO-CALLED
HOT TIPS

stock starts trading. This is a scenario in which there isn't enough stock to satisfy the demand of people wanting to buy-in. The over-subscription factor, coupled with the thought that some of the original subscribers will go back into the open market for another buy, will most likely cause a heavier demand and a **short supply**, thus forcing the stock up.

During the first year of an initial public offering the fundamentals of a company's stock is often ignored; as the "hype" generated by the publicity given the issue seems to **dominate** the open **market setting** on this new issue. After about a year has passed, the investors seem to get back to their senses. They will then start thinking critically of this issue in terms of its financial health, earnings, capitalization and the likelihood of future growth based on its current business plans.

Dealing in new companies is **inherently risky** business, and should only be pursued by those having **venture capital** they can afford to lose. These people know that in buying new issues they are exposed to above-average risks, so they expect above-average returns. In bull markets the new issues often **lead** and may outperform them, whereas in bear markets — watch out! They will be the first to tumble down.

The Securities and Exchange Commission requires that a new company **not make** any new **disclosures** concerning its new issue for a period of 90 days after approval of its **prospectus**. This is known as the **quiet period**. People dealing in new issues look for new disclosures of good news at the end of the quiet period, which can cause a good price jump in the stock, just as bad news may cause a price dip.

GET THE FACTS

BUY THE BEST

FORGET THE REST

SECONDARIES:

These are **distributions** of **stock** in **ongoing** companies that are also known as secondary offerings. The very nature of these already **established** companies with their past business histories open to probing and research by potential investors make these secondaries generally **less risky** than the initial public offerings.

The secondary could be an attempt by a company to raise money for a variety of uses when interest rates are **too high** to borrow directly from banks. The companies would perhaps in this situation prefer to pay 4% to 5% dividends to stockholders, rather than pay 10% to 12% via the then existing prime lending rate at banks.

This distribution may be implimented when a company needs additional funds by applying to the proper state authorities to have its capital stock increased. This permission for additional capital stock becomes the go-ahead signal for a company to sell (distribute) more stock as a fund raiser.

The secondary distribution may also be based on the selling of the company's **treasury stock**. This may be part of the capital stock that was not distributed when the firm started. This undistributed stock becomes treasury stock held by the company and naturally carries **no dividend**. The secondary could be stock that was bought back from stockholders on the

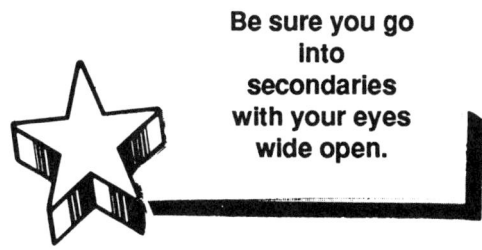

**Be sure you go
into
secondaries
with your eyes
wide open.**

open market when prices were low and dividends were relatively high, only to become treasury stock which may be sold later as a secondary when prices return to the high levels for the anticipated profit. Thus the company would be **speculating** in its **own stock**.

Usually a secondary is a **very large block** of stock, perhaps resulting from the settlement of a large estate, the large holdings of a retiring officer of the company, or some large investor.

The mechanics of selling a secondary is carried on in essentially the same manner as the initial public offerings; that is, by hiring the investment bankers who lead the underwriting group and set up a distribution syndicate of brokers. The security may be **listed** on an exchange, or **unlisted**. The secondaries and the IPOs are generally commission free to the investors; as the start-up company involved generally pays what amounts to a 10% commission to the brokerage people who participate in selling off these offerings in a **timely fashion**.

A broker may act as head underwriter himself if he should have a client that needs to quickly dispose of a large block of stock. The broker may then organize his selling group within his organization, or he may elect to extend the selling efforts to another brokerage unit in order to dispose of the large block. With S.E.C. sanction the underwriting group must undertake to **stabilize the market** in that **stock**, as it proceeds with the new distribution.

Over The Counter Markets

		A indicates also extra above Current Dividend	Stock Symbols		C Payment Accumulated Dividend		Price earnings ratio				
S indicates Stock Dividends							Net change from yesterday's last quote				
							Up $1.50				
365 DAYS							**SALES**				**NET**
HIGH	LOW	STOCK		DIV.	YLD.	PE.	HDS.	HIGH	LOW	LAST	CHG.
43	23 1/4	FAST BUCK CO.	FBU	1.40C	3.8	23	47	29 3/8	28 3/4	29 1/4	+1/2
59	34	SLIM PICKENS INC.	SPK	1.70A	4.0	12	28	42 1/2	39	42	+1 1/2
7 1/2	3 3/4	GREEDY FOOL CO.	GFO	.05S	1.2	3	859	4 1/8	4	4 1/8	+1/8
34 1/4	19 1/2	ROSY PROSPECT INC.	ROP	72E	2.9	12	7	24 3/4	24 3/4	24 3/4	+1/2
8 1/2	3 1/2	BLUE CHIP INC.	BCI	.05G	.8	16	99Z	6 3/4	6 5/8	6 3/4	-
10 1/2	6	PIPE DREAM INC.	PID	WI			3	9	9	9	..
11 5/8	1 3/4	BIG SHARK PARTNERS	BSP	WT			70	3 1/4	3	3	-1/8

E-Paid in preceding 12 months

Dividends in Canadian money

Indicates a warrant or right

When Issued

Z Denotes sales quoted in full

Down 12 1/2 cents

The space problems within the confines of publishing newspapers force some of the publications to "bobtail" their listings. For example: some over-the-counter listings might not list the 365 days high/low, and the percentage yield and price earnings ratio. Some go even further by not reporting the sales and the high and low prices for the day.

Listing Format:

The more complete over-the-counter listings format in most large newspapers are set up in the same arrangement as the listings on the Big Board. However, the trades in this market are carried on to a large extent through the NASDAQ Automated System of the National Association of Securities Dealers. Note that stock symbols have been added by some listings for easy access to news retrieval data bases.

Dividend:

The figure of 1.40 listed in the above illustration next to Fast Buck would represent the payment of accumulated dividends which are in arrears. The 1.40 without the C would simply indicate the annual dividend rate on this stock. Any letter following the dividend or replacing the dividend figure would be "keyed" to an explanation at the bottom of the page on this newspaper stock table.

Sales:

Under the "sales 100's" column of this stock table, the figure of 47 indicates 4700 shares of Fast Buck were traded in this medium on this particular day. (The 2 zeros having been eliminated to conserve space). While odd lots (or less than 100 share lots) are traded in the over-the-counter medium, only the total of full lots would appear on the quotation tables.

Prices:

The prices appearing in the **high/low/last** columns represent the action that took place in the market on the day shown at the top of the listed columns.

Some newspapers will not list securities that trade below $2.00 or under the 1000 share level per day.

These over-the-counter quotations show how trading is reported in the NASDAQ National Market System, which comprises the most **heavily traded** over-the-counter securities.

The prices appearing in the high/low/last columns indicate that investors made purchases as high as the high level, and some purchased or sold as low as the low level. The last sale that occurs is transacted at some price between the high and the low for the day.

The spread for the day on **Fast Buck Co.** in this illustration would be 62 12 cents—the difference between the high and low.

The "net chg" or net change column would be the difference minus or plus between today's last (or closing) price, and yesterday's last price.

The Over-the-Counter Market trades the shares of nearly **5000 companies** through the negotiations of its **market makers**. This is more than **double** the number of companies listed on the Big Board.

Description of Over-The-Counter Market

Unlike the New York and American Stock Exchanges, along with the Regional Auction Exchanges which are actual places of doing business, the over-the-counter market is not a place but a way of doing business in over 40,000 stocks. Also, unlike stock exchange transactions, the prices of which are arrived at by a **Two-Way Auction** system, the over-the-counter stock prices are arrived at by **negotiation** between securities dealers on both sides of the transaction, and between you the customer and your dealer.

"NASDAQ" or the National Association of Securities Dealers Automated Quotation system is the automated quote system developed in the late sixties by the Bunker Ramo Corporation. This is the system now in use by over 4000 dealers in the over-the-counter market operating under the authority of the Securities and Exchange Commission.

NASDAQ has revolutionized the over-the-counter stock business by providing its dealers one **wire-system** that gives exact and instantaneous wholesale price **quotations** from all dealers making markets in the more important over-the-counter stocks.

On Changing Prices

The price of a share of stock may be determined by many circumstances. Some are geared directly to the company such as its earnings, dividends, management, and outlook. Other factors (and at times the overriding elements) are national and may even be international or worldwide in outlook or origin, and may bear no specific connection to your corporation. All of these factors when meshed together is what makes up a stock market. An investor's decision to buy or sell stock reflects the investor's evaluation of the stock's attraction in relation to his or her financial requirements and ownership strategy. All of these varied price opinions are registered continuously on every trading day that stocks are bought and sold.

A listed corporation has just a specified number of shares outstanding to investors. When one buys shares of any stock on an exchange, one must buy from someone else. When you sell, your broker through his organization finds someone who wants to purchase your shares. The exchange provides the market place. Buyers are always competing for the lowest possible price, while sellers compete for the highest price. The stock exchange's job is to have prices arrived at openly, fairly, and reported promptly.

Risk:

While some businesses in a free economy may do very well, others may make only a fair profit, and still others may operate at a loss. Whether or not you invest is a purely personal matter.

Planning an investment program should be based on factual information, for you cannot afford to guess. Some firms may seem to hold promise of substantial growth, while other companies may be the leaders in a comparatively stable industry. The current statistics on some firms may be questionable and suspect—hence the risk.

A comparative "picture" of the risk factor can generally be seen in the price of a stock, hence the need for extra caution and analysis when a stock appears to be a great bargain.

Risk

There is always risk in buying stocks or bonds, and for most individuals the risk looms greater than it should be, because they've never taken the necessary time to study securities in order to invest in them wisely. There is actually a risk in just having money, and as many people realize it's a twofold risk.

The first risk is that you might lose some of your money regardless of what you might do with it. The second risk which is not so apparent is the risk that the money you save today may not buy as much in the future, as prices of goods and services continue to climb in the inflationary spiral.

One can never sidestep this unseen but corrosive risk of inflation. This is the reason why every investment decision you make should take into consideration the two kinds of risk, which are the **obvious** and the **invisible**.

In most forms of investment the greater the return available the greater the risk. You must be prepared to assume the evident risk. The records show that on the average, stocks have paid a **better return** and provided the investor with a better **balance** of protection against the obvious and invisible risks than any other form of investment.

Improving the return over and above the **low** to **no risk** investments such as bank accounts, etc, with the idea of more than offsetting the deterioration of inflationary pressures is what investing in securities is all about.

One way to look at risk in a stock investment is by realizing that it comes in three different forms, namely: **market risk**, **industry risk**, and **company risk.**

Market risk is a measure of the extent to which the average security will be affected by events such as changes in interest rates, inflation trends, and global events, alone with the perceptions, and mass psychology which tie-in to these events.

Industry risk is that of overall risk that is caused by factors which occur with in a specific industry such as labor disputes, obsolete, or shortages of raw materials or products. Also, the industry could be operating in a restrictive regulatory environment.

Company risk is the risk that a company's stock will, over a given period of time rise or fall short of the expected performance, based on the stock's previous relationship to its industry, and the current quality of its management performance.

Both industry and company risk may be managed through Accurate information and diversification, but **market factors cannot.** Therefore, one might be fairly accurate in saying that **market factors** are the **primary** determinants of fluctuations in the value of a diversified portfolio of stocks. In a well diversified portfolio of stocks a good proportion of the uncertainty could be attributed to **market risk factors.**

BREAK INTO YOUR NEWSPAPER - THERE'S A WEALTH OF INFORMATION THERE.

Your Newspaper

The newspaper is your department store of information. You perhaps would not read all that was reported. One would naturally select readings according to one's interests. The financial news is classified accordingly with all investor financial items pulled together into one area of the newspaper. Next to the popularity of the **stock market tables** the feature which commands the greatest numerical **readership following** is said to be the daily descriptive story of the market for that particular day which describes the over-all trends, and the major action **price-wise** that day, along with the purported reasons for the price changes. The morning editions would of course carry the news ticker materials of the previous day.

For financial purposes the choice of a good newspaper carrying the complete story is important, because several hundred newspapers carry a partial list which might prove to be inadequate for the individual. There are approximately 150 newspapers which carry the complete stock listings along with good news coverage. Most good investors realize that "now" is **always** the hardest time to invest, so it doesn't hurt to be **armed** with that greatest amount of information which the **complete newspaper** listing provides.

Strike Price or Exercise Price. Relative to "Calls" this is the Price at which an Option Buyer may Acquire the Underlying Stock from the Option Writer. -Relative to "Puts" this is the Price at which an Option Buyer may Sell (or Put) his Stock to the "Put" Option Writer.

These are the Expiration Months for th which Follow. All Options Expire Third Friday of the Expiration Me

CALLS – LAS

OPTION & N.Y. CLOSE	STRIKE PRICE	MAY
WIDGETS	20	8
23 1/2	22 1/2	1 1/2
23 1/2	25	3/8
23 1/2	30	1/16
GISMO INC.	10	1 1/8
10 7/8	12 1/2	1/16
JUNKIT INC.	15	s
20 5/8	17 1/2	3 3/8
20 5/8	20	1 1/4
20 5/8	22 1/2	5/16
CAPUT CO.	20	3 7/8
23 3/4	22 1/2	1 3/4
23 3/4	25	7/16
23 3/4	30	r
BIG SHOT CO.	35	r
41 1/2	40	2
41 1/2	45	3/16
41 1/2	50	s
MISH MASH INC.	100	14 1/2
114 1/8	105	9 1/2
114 1/8	110	5 1/4
114 1/8	115	2 1/16
PIPE DREAM INC.	35	1 3/8
35 3/8	40	r
35 3/8	45	r
FAST BUCK CO.	70	6 1/2
75 1/2	75	3
75 1/2	80	15/16
75 1/2	85	s

These Widget Call Options are in the Money because the Difference between the Close and Strike Price is greater than these Premium Prices.

This is the Cost of the Option - (or Premium Per Share). Option Contrasts are Generally for 100 Shares of the Underlying Stock. The Premium Today in this Example is $1450 and $500. 14 1/2 x 100 and 5 x 100. The 2 zeros are omitted to conserve space.

April 26th. Stock Price – The Closing Price on the main Exchange for this day on which the Underlying Stock was Traded.

An indication that
Fast Buck Co. Options were
traded at 70 -75 - 80 and 85 dollars

"s" No Cal
Offe

UOTATIONS
STING FOR APRIL 26

**Expiration Months May - June - July
for Put Options**

PUTS – LAST

JULY	MAY	JUNE	JULY
r	r	r	1/2
r	r	r	1
1 1/8	2	r	2 1/2
3/8	r	r	r
1 5/8	3/16	r	9/16
1/2	1 3/4	r	r
r	s	s	3/16
4	r	r	1/2
2 3/8	5/8	r	1 1/2
1 1/4	r	r	2 5/8
4 1/4	1/16	3/16	1/4
2 5/16	5/16	5/8	15/16
1 1/8	1 1/2	2	2 5/16
3/16	r	r	r
7	1/16	3/16	3/8
2 7/8	9/16	1	1 5/8
13/16	3 5/8	r	r
1/4	s	s	r
15 1/2	1/4	s	15/16
11	5/8	1 3/16	1 3/4
7 3/4	1 1/2	2 9/16	3 1/4
5	3 3/8	4 5/8	5 1/2
2	1	r	r
1/2	r	r	r
1/16	r	s	r
r	1/2	r	2
5 1/4	1 7/8	r	r
2 3/4	r	r	7
1 11/16	s	s	r

On April 26th, $262.50 is the cost of a Junkit Inc. 22 1/2 Put Option Expiring the 3rd Friday in July.

These May Mish Mash Inc. Puts are in the Money because the Difference between the Close and Strike Price is Greater than these Premiums.

"r" Put Options Not Traded

"s" Put Options Offered

Basic Details of Option Trading

The listed option quotations in your newspaper which emanate from the major exchanges are **rights** which the purchaser of the option has, to buy or to sell an **underlying** security (generally a stock) at a stated price, within a stated period of time. It should be understood that because of the time element, the option is a wasting away asset as time "rolls" along and its expiration date approaches.

If the underlying stock of a call option has not increased in price by the expiration date, the value of the buy option is zero to the potential buyer, and the writer of the call option will have pocketed that call premium .

The right which is given by the option is paid for by the buyer of the option. The writer of the option receives this premium money whether or not the option is exercised. Each option is generally for 100 shares of a specific underlying security which is widely held, and actively traded .

The option striking prices for equity options are generally introduced at 2 1/2 point intervals for stocks trading below $25.00, at 5 point intervals for stocks trading from $25.00 to $300.00, and at 10 point intervals for those stocks trading above $300.00.

Premium:
The outstanding consideration (if there is one) about options is the **premium** or **cost** of the "call" or "put."

Many buyers try to purchase options when the premiums are low, and try later to sell them as their prices are propelled upward in the market place when the underlying stock on the major exchanges increases in value.

Other buyers will hold their options as their strategy dictates allowing the stock to increase in price. When the difference between the exercise price and the close price exceeds the premium price, the owner has a built in paper profit. The option at this point in time is said to be "in-the-money," and exercising the call at this time would enable the option buyer to purchase the stock at the exercise price. The option buyer then sells his recently purchased stock at the current close price to realize his **actual** profit.

Commissions:
One must not of course overlook commissions in all of these operations. These commissions take their "toll" and are not reflected on a newspaper

option listing. Therefore if the option owners strategy is to buy the underlying stock by exercising his option right, the difference between the exercise price and the closing price should be somewhat more than the cost of the option premium to allow for the cost of the commissions and the intended profit.

The reverse applies to "put" options where the buyer of this option believes that the price of the underlying stock will fall **far enough** below the difference between the strike (or exercise) and the close price to more than offset his option premium plus commissions.

Monetary Importance of Premium:

The monetary importance of the **premium** in the option market is of paramount importance to both the buyers and the sellers, and this raises the interesting question — of what factors determine the amount and changes in the cost of option premiums.

Looking again at the "sample news option listing" one may observe that the cost of a premium is not exactly the difference between **the strike and the close price**. The increase in price of most premiums over and above the difference in price between the exercise price and the closing price is in some measure a reflection of the supply and demand pressures of the market place. Traders in options are generally more anxious to buy call options at times of rising stock prices. However, stock owners (which are option writers) become less interested during these same times in writing calls, and more interested in outright ownership of stocks to enable their participation in the "run-up" of their stock for a capital gain. One may readily see that the opposing self interest of these two groups, the **buyers** and **writers** of options, all other factors being equal has a tendency of raising the cost level of options. Thus in a market environment of rising stock prices when call option writers are fewer in number, all else being equal the premiums will tend to command high prices.

With the above in mind the reverse mathematics would apply to put options. When stock prices are strong the demand would normally reduce for "puts" and therefore generate weak premium prices for puts. A weakness in stock prices however would normally increase demand for puts and therefore firm-up prices for this type option.

Factors Affecting Premium Prices:

While various factors affect the prices of option premiums, the following are several which tend to be of major significance.

1. The **relationship** between the exercise price (or strike price) and the current market price of the underlying stock.

2. The **time factor** naturally affects option premiums because all other factors being equal the more time left until the expiration date the higher the premium will tend to be.

3. The volatility (or up and down tradability) of the underlying security is also a major factor. Stocks which tend to fluctuate a great deal will be the underlying stock of higher priced option premiums. The reverse will be true of stocks normally trading in a narrow price range.

Parity:

When an option reaches **parity** price the premium will most probably move point for point right along with the underlying stock. Parity occurs for a call when the addition of the premium and exercise price becomes equal to the market price of the stock.

Parity occurs for a put however, when the premium cost subtracted from the exercise price equals the price of the underlying stock.

Before reaching parity, premiums tend not to move in unison with stock prices.

Because many options are purchased for their leverage quality, rising premiums will result in reduced leverage which causes the option to be less attractive to buyers.

As an illustration to the prior statement if the price of a stock is $60.00 and the option is $5.00 the buyer's leverage is 12 to 1. But if the price of the option were to go up $1.00 following a $1.00 increase in the stock price the leverage would be reduced to 10 to 1. Higher premiums of course require heavier capital outlays and tends to reduce demand for the option. When a stock price rises from $60.00 to $61.00 the percentage increase is only 1.6%, but if the call option rises from $5.00 to $6.00 the percentage increase to the buyer is 20%, and so is the risk factor.

Time Factor:

Because options are on a decreasing time table to the expiration date so far as the exercising of the option right is concerned, the time factor, expiring as it does is another element which tends to offset the tendency of an option to change value in the same measure as stock prices. A good example of this would be that a three week uptrend in stock prices would most probably not be fully reflected in the increased prices of option premiums, and a partial reason for this lies in the fact that the options in the above example would be three weeks closer to the expiration date.

OPTIONS:
A legal contract that gives the holder the **right** to buy or sell a precise amount of an underlying interest (generally a stock), at a fixed price that is called the **exercise** or **strike price**; providing the transaction is consummated within the **specified time** allowed by the contract.

OPTION BUYER:
The option buyer obtains the right imparted by the option. This put or call option buyer is also referred to as the **holder**.

OPTION WRITER:
Also referred to as the **option seller**, is obligated to fullfill the terms of the option. This is done by surrendering his interest in the **asset** (generally a stock) if and when he is **assigned an exercise**.

EXERCISE PRICE:
The price at which a **call option** buyer has the right to **purchase** the underlying interest. Relative to a **put option**—the price at which the buyer of the put option has the right to **sell** the underlying interest.

HOW T0 EXERCISE:
A U.S. type option may be exercised any time from the day it was purchased until the last day before it expires. In order to exercise the option the holder must ask the broker to give the exercise instructions to the Options Clearing Corporation. To have the option exercised on a **specific day**, the holder must ask the broker to exercise before the broker's **cut-off time** for entering exercise instructions on that specific day. Different brokers have **different** cut-off times for accepting exercise instructions from customers, and the cut-offs could differ for **different classes** of options.

PREIMIUMS:
Premiums for stock options are expressed in the number of **dollars** per share. These dollars must be multiplied by the total **number of shares** of the underlying stock covered by the option in order to determine the **cost** of the **option**.

DIVIDENDS:
The writer of a covered call option retains the cash dividends declared on the underlying stock during the time **before** the option is exercised. However, the call holder is entitled to the dividend if he or she exercises the option before the **ex-dividend date**.

IN THE MONEY:
This is a term indicating that, at the current market price of the underlying interest (in this case a stock) an option has some **intrinsic value**. This value is the amount by which the option is considered to be **in the money**.

OUT OF THE MONEY:
This happens when the exercise price of a call is **higher** than the current market price of the underlying stock, or when the exercise price of a put option is **lower** than the current market price of the underlying interest. The option is out of the money by the **difference between** these **two prices**.

AT THE MONEY:
When the market price of an underlying interest is **equal** to the exercise price of an option.

COVERED CALL WRITER:
This is a call option writer who **actually owns** the underlying interest that will be deliverable to the option buyer if and when the buyer elects to exercise the option.

UNCOVERED CALL WRITER:
This call writer has greater **risk exposure** than the covered call writer since this writer does not currently own the underlying interest, nor an option that **might offset** this writer's loss should the option buyer exercise his privilege when his option is in the money. This uncovered, (or naked) option writer would be operating on **margin**, and must have ready liquid assets that he or she can afford to lose. There must be **sufficient margin** in the naked option writers margin account to cover the purchase of the underlying security for delivery to the option buyer when the **call is exercised**.

STANDARDIZED OPTIONS:

The Chicago Board Options Exchange, Inc. that began operations in 1973 has caused listed options to become popular investment vehicles for certain investors seeking **profit, protection,** and **risk transference**.

This exchange is the second largest securities exchange in the U.S., and is the world's largest options exchange. Also, the CBOE deals only in option trading. Here, options are traded on the common stock of more major public companies than on any other options exchange.

The Standardized Options discussed here are **put** and **call options** issued by the Options Clearing Corporation (OCC). However, put and call options are presently available covering the **underlying interests** of common stocks, stock indexes, foreign currencies, and debt securities. Who knows? The need may develop for trading on options of other types of underlying interests.

Many of the risks involved in trading options are similar for all types of options. However, some type options may have **special risks** that apply exclusively to those options.

This book tries only to very basically describe what options are all about, but does not attempt to present a detailed description of all the technical provisions governing standardized options. Also, this book does not describe the **many rules** that govern the form and behavioral action of option trading. These rules differ somewhat from one market to another, and may from time to time undergo change of necessity; as experience and progress changes are needed as determined by the Options Clearing Corporation which is subject to regulation by the U.S. Securities and Exchange Commission.

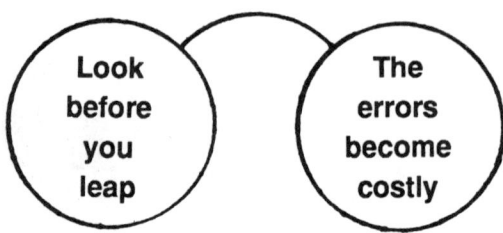

Look
before
you
leap

The
errors
become
costly

Additionally, this book cannot get into the many strategies which perhaps run into the many hundreds, and the choice of which depend on a particular investor's need and investment objectives.

Unless an investor is willing to learn what options are, how they work, and just exactly what risks are associated with specific strategies—then better to forget 'em; as these are not securities like some common stocks of the Blue Chip variety where some investors would choose to "buy 'em and forget'em". The **short life** of options does not allow for this "laisser-faire" attitude on the part of the investor.

There are many books and publications in libraries and bookstores dealing extensively in **option strategies**—those strategies and tactics needed by you the investor as they apply to your specific needs. Finally, various markets and brokerage operations also have **good materials** available to the investors.

The Options Clearing Corp. plays the role of **Guarantor** of all **option transactions,** and as such places an option buyer in a position of relying on the back-up system set up by OCC rather than rely on any specific option writer for fullfilling his or her end of the transaction. The obligation of option writers to the clearing corporation is **guaranteed** by the brokerage "Clearing Members " that carry the accounts of writers or their brokers .

All the Chicago equity options expire on the Saturday that follows the third Friday of the month in which the option is due to expire. The trading activity of options is carried on by brokers in somewhat the same way as the orders they execute to buy and sell stocks for their clients. Unlike the trading of stocks that are evidenced by stock certificates, the trading activity in options is evidenced only by the **printed statements** of the various brokerage firms handling the transactions.

ABOUT INDEX OPTIONS:

Index options which are fairly recent popular innovations in risk transference began in 1983. Unlike stock options which, when exercised have an **underlying stock** as the "prize" or end result that may prvide a profit, the **index options** will permit investors to take positions on the **market as a whole** based on how strongly the investors feel concerning the general or immediate trend of the market itself.

An investor who believes that the stock market is headed upward may be interested in buying **a call index option**, whereas an investor entertaining the belief that stocks are trending down would perhaps be interested in buying a **put index option**.

An index is a measure of worth covering a **group of stocks** or other interests that is generally expressed in harmony to a **base** that was established when the index was begun. Stock indexes may be set-up in different ways. Some indexes are **"value weighted,"** which means that in computing the index value, the market price of each component stock is multiplied by the number of shares out-standing. This method of calculating the index will cause **larger corporations** to exert a greater **influence** on the price level of this type index than the price changes that occur at the smaller corporations within the index.

An index may be created to represent an entire stock market, an industry such as the **utilities**, a large segment of the market such as the **industrials**, or it may be constructed to represent a **particular market**. An index may be weak or strong based on its underlying features.

An investor who intends to trade in index options should be aware of the basic features of the chosen index, including the way it is constructed. This information may be easily obtained from the exchange or a broker that deals in the particular index.

Trading option prices are updated continuously during a trading day, and index activity is reported at various intervals. Brokers can supply current index levels, and closing values are published in large newspapers on a daily basis.

When an **index option** is exercised the settlement is done by a **payment of cash**, and not by the delivery of stock, as in the case of a stock option. The assigned writer in this situation is required to pay the exercising holder cash dollars equivalent to the difference between the exercise settlement value of the underlying index on the day the exercise is tendered to the Clearing Corporation, and the exercise price of the option; multiplied by a specific multiplier which was determined when the index originated.

A **multiplier** performs a function that corresponds to the **unit of trading** for a stock option. Different option indexes could have different multipliers, so investors should know their applicable multiplier.

Example:
Let's suppose a holder of a June 70 call on a specific index decides to exercise it on a day when the (striking) exercise settlement value of the index is determined to be $75.00. Let's further assume that the **multiplier** for options on this specific index is 100. The assigned writer would then be required to pay, and the exercising holder would qualify to receive $500 in cash.

$$(75-70) \times 100 = \$500$$

Mutual Fund Listing Explanations

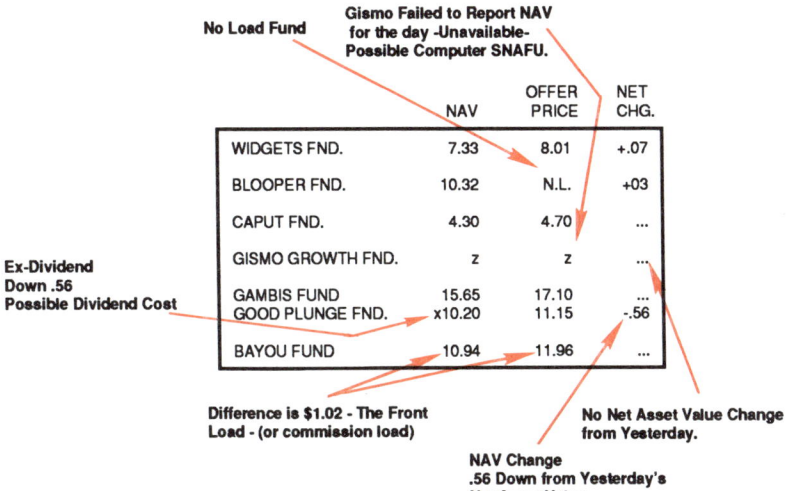

No Load Fund

Gismo Failed to Report NAV
for the day -Unavailable-
Possible Computer SNAFU.

Ex-Dividend
Down .56
Possible Dividend Cost

	NAV	OFFER PRICE	NET CHG.
WIDGETS FND.	7.33	8.01	+.07
BLOOPER FND.	10.32	N.L.	+03
CAPUT FND.	4.30	4.70	...
GISMO GROWTH FND.	z	z	...
GAMBIS FUND	15.65	17.10	...
GOOD PLUNGE FND.	x10.20	11.15	-.56
BAYOU FUND	10.94	11.96	...

Difference is $1.02 - The Front
Load - (or commission load)

NAV Change
.56 Down from Yesterday's
Net Asset Value.

No Net Asset Value Change
from Yesterday.

NAV--OFFER PRICE--NAV CHANGE
NAV:

The heading "NAV" which stands for "Net Asset Value" is generally figured by the fund managers at the fund's office once or twice a day. "NAV" is computed by multiplying today's market price (on the exchange or over-the-counter) by the total of the various securities currently in today's portfolio. One must now bear in mind that the fund most probably bought and sold securities since yesterday, hence the inventory of the fund's securities in the portfolio may change from day to day.

Generally the last fund computation every day takes place after the exchanges close. The fund's purchases for the day are added to the portfolio, and the sales are deducted. Also, current expenses and liabilities are deducted. This produces the new days new asset value of the entire portfolio, which is then divided by the fund shares outstanding to its investors to produce the "NAV" or net asset value per share found in the newspaper listings.

Offer Price:

The column headed offer price— is simply the addition of the "NAV" or net asset value of the portfolio to the "front load" or commission load which covers commissions to salespeople, and all other distribution costs.

The "NL" designations in this offer price column stands for "No Load," and signifies a no load, or no commission fund. The "NL" designated funds do business by mailings, and advertising, but do not rely on salespeople to generate business activity.

NAV Chg:

The column headed "NAV change" — is the difference between today and yesterday's NAV change as figured in the "NAV" explanation. In the case of a mutual fund carrying a front load, the "NAV change" would be the difference between today and yesterdays offer price. The "NAV change" in either case generally reflects how well or how poorly the fund portfolio did in the open market since the previous day.

Investors should be cognizant of the fact that when they buy stocks in the open market, commissions are charged investors by their brokers on the buy and the selling side, whereas in dealing with a front load fund the commission though seemingly high is paid only on the buy into the fund.

Mutual Fund Defined:

A mutual fund can be described simply as a pooling of the money of shareholders who are willing in effect to hire professionals to buy and sell securities for them.

Advantages of Mutual Funds:

1. The pooling of resources enable the fund to **diversify broadly**. While an investor might buy two or three stocks with his investment dollars, the fund would perhaps have a diversified portfolio of stocks involving 100 to 150 different companies. The net effect of diversification is that of reducing risk.

2. The fund relieves the investor of the chore of selecting among thousands of stocks on the several markets, and the investor is also relieved of the time consuming job of following up on (or keeping tabs on) his investments. These important operations are performed by the professional staff at the fund's offices which is monitoring the market place at all times.

3. There is never a problem in selling (or redeeming) the mutual fund owner's shares. The funds stand ready to buy back its own shares at any given time, which makes a mutual fund investment **almost** as **liquid** as a bank deposit.

Mutual funds offer various other advantages but diversification, professional management, and liquidity are the main ones.

Investment Trusts:
This type company uses its capital for investment in other companies.

The two types of investment trusts are: the **closed end**, which sells its shares on the open markets and the share price of which is determined by the auction and over-the-counter trading climate, and the second type is the **mutual funds** where the fund share price is determined daily based on the net asset value of the fund's portfolio.

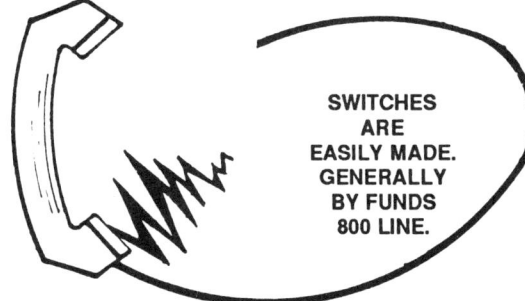

SWITCHES ARE EASILY MADE. GENERALLY BY FUNDS 800 LINE.

YOU HAVEN'T LOOKED INTO MUTUALFUNDS - HOW EMBARRASSING!

WHAT IS A MUTUAL FUND?

A mutual fund is classified as a financial service organization that obtains monies fromm its shareholders, and by investing these pooled funds will work hard to make them grow and will agree to pay its shareholders their monies on demand for the ongoing value of their investments.

The investors who join a specific fund have essentially the same investment needs, and they are actually placing their dollars in the hands of professional investing managers who will invest their clients monies in various stocks, bonds, and other securities or assets that in their best judgement will return the required dividends and profits—to be distributed to the investor's account in the ratio that the investor has committed his monies to the total of all assets in the mutual fund's portfolio.

When an investor buys shares in a mutual fund, he or she is actually pooling his or her investment monies with other investors to obtain an equity interest in a wide variety of stocks and bonds, or other profit producing assets.

Most of the mutual funds will offer their shares to the general public on a continuous basis; and because they issue shares continuously and redeem them the same way, they are sometimes called "open-ended" investment companies. Some might call them "open-ended investment trusts." These last two terms will serve to differentiate them from the "closed-end" investment companies that operate stock companies, some of which list on the major stock exchanges, and whose total capital stock outstanding is "free-floating" among interested investors who buy and sell on one of the national auction markets, or in the over-the-counter market.

If your attention span to "husbanding" your float cash is not that great, or if you just lack the time or inclination to keep careful watch of your investment portfolio, why not get into a fund, and have access to professional invest-

ALL FUNDS ARE
NOT CREATED
EQUAL

MUTUAL FUNDS -
LET'S DISCUSS
IT.

ment managers who operate realistically speaking at a very low fee which is made possible of course by the hugh pool of monies under one efficient management operation.

WHAT IS A MONEY MARKET FUND?

Money market funds are generally designed to maximize current income while protecting the invested capital from possible erosion. By pooling the cash of thousands of investors seeking high yields and daily liquidity, these money market trusts provide appropriate and practical ways for individuals as well as institutional investors to share in America's gigantic money market, where transactions typically involving $1,000,000 and up are very commonplace. These funds offer attractive alternatives for those who prefer not to tie-up their funds in savings certificates where time of cash in deposit is an essential element of the good return; or where lower yields are unacceptable whether from savings accounts or other lower return investments.

Money market funds invest their fundholder's monies in such things as certificates of deposit of the major U.S. banks, short term securities issued by the U.S. Treasury and agencies of the U.S. Government, prime commercial paper, high quality short-term corporate obligations, negotiable certificates of deposit, and bankers acceptances of major U.S. banks. Some money funds even deal in the above type securities issued by foreign banks and governments. The "stock in trade" of the money funds is interest payments which they receive on short term debt instruments which they hold in their portfolios, and on which they seek to obtain maximum current income.

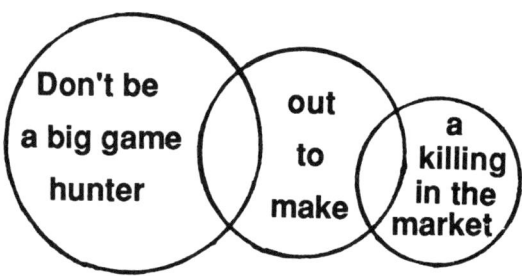

Money market funds become an excellent "parking place" for cash when their current return is high as a reflection of high interest rates. When interest rates subside and venture capital companies start using the lower rental monies, great amounts of cash will move from the money market funds into growth stocks, and growth stock funds to enable the investor to participate in the newly perceived and anticipated growth which generally results partially from the corporate opportunity. (The rental of money is a great expense to Industrial America.)

HOW DO THE MUTUAL FUNDS MAKE THEIR MONEY FOR THE FUNDHOLDERS?

Mutual funds make their money in basically the same three ways that an individual might profit. They may buy with the dividend consideration in mind. They also buy into companies whose stock is expected to rise in price as positive profit producing developments occur within those industrial or commercial companies.

Some funds will buy for quick sales at higher prices than the buy costs as economic and non economic factors in the markets propel stocks upward based on the real or fancied expectations of the investors at the stock and bond markets. This buying would be done for quick turnover in the short and intermediate swings which occur at the exchanges.

TOGETHERNESS HAS
CREATED A STAGGERING
FORCE IN WORLD
FINANCE.

WHAT IS A GROWTH MUTUAL FUND?

This is a diverified investment company that buys and trades primarily in common stocks and may trade at times in securities convertible into common stocks such as convertible bonds, convertible perferred stocks, and warrants (which are rights) to purchase common stocks. These funds generally seek long-term growth of capital for the fundholders, and dividend income is only incidental as an objective.

The common stocks in the portfolio are chosen mainly on the basis of greater-than-average earnings growth potential, and much attention is given to the quality of management in company stocks being purchased. Some growth funds will purchase growth stocks in groupings and establish by policy a specific percentage of their funds (like 20%) to be invested in each of these "tiers". This tier strategy might comprise of established growth, emerging growth, cyclical growth, and special situations growth stocks.

WHAT IS A BALANCED FUND?

The balanced mutual fund is one which has as its main investment objective the minimizing of investment risk, and at the same time attempting to provide long-term growth and some current income.

Over the years the balanced funds looked to accomplish their mission by holding at all times a portfolio proportion of about 20 percent to 50 percent senior securities (bonds or preferred stocks), and roughly 50 percent in common stocks. These funds try to hold common stocks which do not carry much risk, but do have some growth possibilities, and preferred stock and/ or possibily bonds which generally carry no appreciable risk but also no growth possibilities because of course they are fixed income securities.

These balanced funds have had quite a good pefrormance record over the years. They generally do not yield as much as the "bond" or "income" funds though they are thought to normally out-perform the "growth" funds. Balanced funds are but a small segment of the total funds in operation.

WHAT IS A MUNICIPAL BOND FUND?

A municipal bond fund is a diversified management investment company whose main objective is obtaining a high level of current income which would be exempt from Federal taxes through the purchase of municipal bonds and notes which are federally tax exempt fixed income securities issued by municipalities such as: states, counties, cities, towns, villages, authorities, and districts throughout the country.

These municipal bonds carry a rating arrived at by the major rating services, and in effect these are not unlike the ratings assigned to the commercial and industrial bonds given regular corporate America; and which are primarily the holdings of regular "high yield funds".

WHAT ARE SPECIALIZED FUNDS?

This is a relatively small but growing number of funds that concentrate their investments in a confined number of industries. They may invest in the stocks of utility companies, or bank shares of stocks of South African gold mines. Some specialize in Canadian stocks, or government securities. The latest entrants to expand this group of funds specialize in computer stocks, and drug company stocks. Some specialized funds now concentrate strictly on communication stocks, while some trade in domestic gold and silver mines. One fund even concentrates in aviation.

The management people in specialized funds have highly trained personnel in their chosen field of activity and they believe their concentration gives them an edge over the theory of investing in the market as a whole.

WHAT IS A CAPITAL GAINS FUND?

This is a type of fund that is difficult to describe exactly because many of them take such widely varied routes to accomplish their mission of maximum capital gains. All of the methods used by these funds to maximize capital gains are higher on the risk-reward scale than most funds in view of the make-up of these policies that call for taking above average risks to achieve their maximum capital gains.

These funds would be obligated to clearly reveal in their prospectus the chancy procedures used to maximize their capital gains. Also, the shareholder sales pitch and other reports put out be the fund would tend to elaborate on the methods used for their anticipated success.

MUTUAL FUNDS - IMPROVING YOUR BOTTOM LINE IS THEIR TOP PRIORITY.

WHAT IS AN INCOME FUND?

This is a mutual fund that invests in well established companies paying good dividends, and which relies more on these high and hopefully sure dividends for their normal gains distributions to the investors in the fund.

This is the type fund that is especially good for those investors who want stability and a steady income. However, in a rapidly expanding economy the investor in the income fund would most likely sacrifice some nice capital gains distributions for that safe and steady income which perhaps would not match the earning of the growth fund. The key element here of course would be "timing," as to whether or not we were in a period of accelerated expansion of the general economy.

WHAT IS A HIGH YIELD FUND?

The high yield fund is generally a management investment company that concentrates its investment efforts on fixed income securities such as: bonds, debentures, and notes which are rated no lower than "B" by the two major security rating services.

Capital appreciation is a secondary objective with the high yield funds, and this objective is sought only when it's consistent with the primary objective which provides the high yield. Some capital appreciation could show up in a high yield fund from an improvement in the credit rating of an issuer's securities being held in the fund's portfolio, or from the effect of a general lowering of interest rates in the economy. The reverse could happen as capital depreciation results for example: from a lowered credit standing by the rating services, or a general rise in interest rates. The fulfillment of the fund's objectives will depend greatly upon the adviser's analytical and portfolio managment skill, and there are no assurances that the required objectives will be achieved.

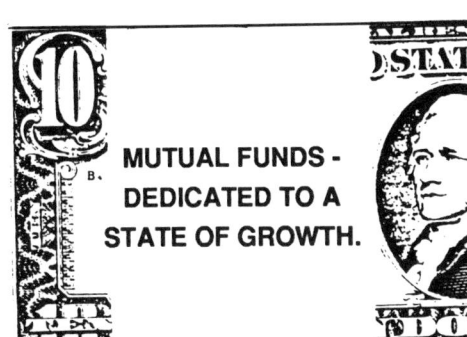

MUTUAL FUNDS -
DEDICATED TO A
STATE OF GROWTH.

MUTUAL FUNDS - GIVE YOU
A WIDE FREEDOM OF CHOICE
AND FREEDOM OF CHANGE.

IS IT GOOD TO COMPARE MUTUAL FUNDS?

Certainly it's good, but they must be compared fairly to have worth while meaning. One cannot compare the average mutual fund on the basis of a short time-span, such as a year. The fund having a bad comparison this year may have an outstanding record long term. Therefore, if a comparison is made, it should cover at least 8 to 10 years to convey an accurate picture of results.

The "long-term" gain when added to the current "annual payout" would be the proper way to make worthwhile comparisons. Comparing an income fund to a growth fund would be like comparing apples and cucumbers. The growth fund, though having every appearance of being hot in its prospects, may own an over supply of issues involving chance, luck, risk, and unpredictability. The income fund on the other hand may not appear as a glamour fund, but may be heavily committed to basic leading issues paying fairly good and steady dividends, or interest payments, and which are not frought with "costly surprises."

In recapping— the average investor should guard against chasing around from one fund to another simply on the basis of the latest year's results. Remember! that except for money market funds the great majority of funds are for long-term consideration. There are plenty of better places to invest for short term.

WHEN LOOKING AT A NEWSPAPER TABLE, HOW DOES ONE KNOW WHICH ARE LOAD (THOSE CHARGING A COMMISSION) FUNDS, AND WHICH ARE NO-LOAD (THOSE CHARGING NO COMMISSION)?

The price on a newspaper price listing tells the story. If the bid price is $14.02 and the asked price is $15.85, the difference of $1.83 is the commission and therefore the "load" indication on this fund. If the bid and asked price were both listed as $14.02, this would be the indicator of a "no-load" (no commission) fund.

There are roughly two catagories of load funds, those straight load funds which charge commissions on all sales as they occur during the entire life of the account; and the front load funds that normally charge a commission equivalent in value to 50% up-front of the first year's payment into the fund.

The quitting of a straight load fund would be no problem, as excessive commissions would not have been paid. However, the quitting of a front-load contractual plan within five years would most probably entail a loss because commissions paid (up-front) would have been intended to cover an extended length of the contract covering ten years or more.

HOW CAN I TELL HOW WELL MY MUTUAL FUND IS DOING.

By being aware of the three profit elements: 1--by watching the dividend payouts which the fund sends you. 2--by watching for the amount of capital gains which will be distributed to you by the fund. 3--by being aware of the net asset value of your shares at any given time. This is the NAV figure which appears in the daily financial tables of newspapers, and is the actual buy and sell figure of the fund shares on the days they appear in these financial columns.

The difference between (the redemption) sales value of a fund's shares and the value of the shares when purchased, would represent an undistributed capital gain or loss depending on whether the shares were redeemed for more or less than when purchased.

Funds do not allow their fundholders to be ill-informed on their operations. The Federal and State laws require full disclosure of a fund's financial condition. This includes quarterly, semi-annual, and annual reports for many funds. It also includes performance reports, financial statements, and a list of securities which make up their portfolio along with any other pertinent information of interest to the fundholders.

HOW DOES ONE BUY A NO-LOAD (NO COMMISSION) FUND?

All sales of no-load funds are produced by direct mailings and by newspaper and magazine advertising. Potential investors should write several funds asking for their purchase form and prospectus. This enables the investor to make comparisons of various fund plans to see which fund operates in the style which best fits his needs.

MUTUAL FUNDS - A FINE CAPITALIST BUZZWORD FOR LONG-TERM BENEFITS

TOGETHERNESS HAS CREATED A STAGGERING FORCE IN WORLD FINANCE.

WHAT ABOUT CLOSED-END INVESTMENT COMPANIES? (NOT MUTUALS)

These are investment companies the shares of which are traded on the major stock exchanges. The prices of these shares are basically related to asset value, but in a very real sense the on-going share prices are related to supply and demand of the stocks, based on relative values placed on such stocks in the market place by the competing buyers and sellers at the "auction block". (the market place)

The current price of a stock in a closed-end investment company would therefore be the final appraisial of the last buyer and seller at the "auction post." The internal operations of these investment companies are carried on in much the same manner as the open-ended mutuals insofar as investing the monies are concerned. However, unlike the mutual funds, no monies have to held by the closed-end investment companies for the active redemptions of shares. Hence, these companies may conceivably be more fully invested at any given time. The mutuals would be forced by law to keep a sufficient amount to cash on hand to pay off current demand redemptions by the investors in the fund who might "want out" at any given time. We must remember of course that with the mutuals, the fund shares may be redeemed at current net asset value at any time, making the mutuals just about as liquid as a bank account.

The closed-end stock companies do not continually issue or redeem stock as do the mutuals; for theirs is a fixed capitalization like that of any other industrial or commercial firm having listing a on a Stock Exchange.

ABOUT
50%
OF MUTUALS
GIVE YOU
800 LINE
PHONE
SERVICE

MUTUAL FUNDS -
THEY'VE GOT WHAT
YOU NEED TO
SUCCEED.

Their capitalization is based mainly on a stock portfolio instead of hard assets such as inventories, equipment, machinery, cash, or buildings etc. Their business of course is that of investing as opposed to perhaps manufacturing, merchandising, banking or transportation.

If a closed-end fund (also known as a closed-end investment trust) investor wanted to sell his 1000 shares of "Super Duper" fund that has a capitalization of 1,000,000 shares outstanding, he would of course be selling part or that million share block. The availability of such shares on the open market is strictly based on the willingness of some share owners to sell. The one million share capitalization would never change except for a rare possible offering of a new issue by the closed-end fund to expand its capitalization enabling expansion of its portfolio.

The open-ended strictly mutual funds are not confined to fixed capitalizations. The monies at their disposal varies continuously as buying pressure for its shares increases or decrease. When an investor purchases shares in a mutual fund, the fund receives this new infusion of capital, and the action of issuing new shares to an investor automatically increases its capitalization. When this investor (fundholder) sells his open-ended shares, they are redeemed by the fund, or retired. (Think of them as being discarded.) They do not transfer from seller to buyer as they do in the closed-end funds. The number of outstanding shares in an open-ended fund may increase or decrease, and this all depends on whether investors are adding or withdrawing money more heavily.

A selling run on an open-ended mutual could possibly exhaust the cash on hand which is ordinarily used for redemptions. If this should occur the fund would sell some of its portfolio assets to satisify any further selling demands from its fundholders.

WHAT'S MORE IMPORTANT THAN PRICE? SOMETIMES, IT'S WHO BUYS YOUR PORTFOLIO OF SECURITIES.

WHAT ARE THE EXPENSE ELEMENTS INVOLVED IN DEALING WITH THE MUTUAL FUNDS.

The mutual fund investor may normally look forward to three cost elements. The "management fee" which is the cost charged by the adviser (or managing firm) for the services rendered in managing the fund's portfolio. The terms, conditions, and cost of the management fees are normally outlined in the prospectus.

The second cost is the sales (or commission) charge. There is naturally a cost of marketing most any product today and mutual funds are no exception. The sales people selling funds put a good measure of effort into this service type occupation, and their commission is the result of their effort in getting the fund's shares sold to the proper customers. The front-load sales or commission charge is the most important, especially when thinking short term. Commission details are outlined in the prospectus, but if the commission is a lump sum; for example, $800.00 on an initial sale of $10,000 worth of fund shares, it's not considered a high commission if through appreciation resulting from the reinvestment of the dividends and distributions the same $10,000 is worth $25,000 or more in ten years.

Initially, the $800.00 commission would most probably be deducted from the $10,000, so that only $9200 would effectively be invested. One may easily see here that funds have to be considered for long-term investments only. The foregoing example of the $800 front-load commission sale clearly shows that the consideration of selling out the shares in three or four years

MUTUAL FUNDS - THEY WILL OFFER YOU A STRATEGY FOR LONG-TERM INVESTMENT OPPORTUNITY AND FINANCIAL SECURITY

without a heavy loss would be unthinkable in view of the high percentage loss which the $800 lost on the commissions would be relative to the $9,200 initial investment. This loss would be greater of course if the funds profits were lean for those three or four years.

Inexperienced investors sometimes think in terms of a 6%, 8%, or 9% commission as being too high. However, the commission may only be considered too high relative to what is received long term on the sale of the fund shares, and in the above example if a total of $25,000 is received by sale time, the commission percentage of $800 to $35,000 (the cost of the round trip in the market) would be about 2.3%. This commission of $800 is perhaps no higher than the total commission which would be generated by stock broker in a buy situation of $10,000 and a subsequent sell situation ten years later of $25,000 worth of any given stock on the open market. Be that as it may——one may readily see here that the caliber and competency of management is one of the most important factors in determining whether to go with a no-load fund, or front-load mutual fund.

The third and least important cost component of the fund could be termed operating expenses. Such expenses would include rent, taxes, printing expenses, travel, auditing fees, custodial fees charged by banks, legal fees, and office expenses such as paper and paper clips etc. These operating expenses would most likely total less than one percent of the portfolio assets.

Municipal Bond Funds For Safe Convenient Tax-Free Income

THE KIND OF STUFF THAT PROVIDES FOR GOOD RETIREMENTS

MUTUAL FUNDS - IN THE KNOWLEDGE BUSINESS OF INVESTING.

WHAT IS A MUTUAL FUND PROSPECTUS?

The mutual fund prospectus is an accurate description of the financial product to be sold. While they are not all models of clarity in every repect as one tries to read and understand them, they do provide the investor the required information mandated by various Acts of Congress, and set forth in U.S. Code Title 80A-15.

The prospectus is the work of lawyers attempting to define the prodcuct, and their work on a prospectus is reviewed carefully by the Securities and Exchange Commission that gives final approval as to accuracy of the prospectus relative to the operation of the fund in question. The differences in prospectusses will therefore be the result of the differences in the makeup of funds, and how the various Federal and State laws come into play to effect an accurate presentation of the fund operations.

The following list is an outline of the various headings and subheadings of paragraphs which may appear in most prospectusses. These headings give a good indication of the assortment of information given to the investor in the prospectus. Some variations would occur in the format of some prospectusses depending on the type of fund. The asterisk * will indicate those paragraphs which are perhaps the most important from the standpoint of investor research. These will be elaborated upon as we get to them on the list.

      1. - Synopsis of the fund- or highlighting- or summary.
          (Generally a thumbnail sketch of the prospectus.)

     *2. - Pershare income and capital changes.
         (#2 in importance)

MAKE YOUR EFFORT, AND SOMEONE WILL SHOW YOU HOW.

3. - Calculation of yield.
   Dividends—(For money market funds)

4. - Calculation of offering price.
   (Especially on municipals)

* 5. - Investment objectives and policies. (#1 in importance)
   Portfolio strategies - (Growth funds)

6. - Municipal bonds and notes.

7. - Portfolio turnover.

8. - Portfolio management.

* 9. - Investment restrictions. - (#3 in importance)
   Generally 15 to 20 restrictions on what the fund
   will not do as a matter of policy or law.

10. - List of officers and directors, or trustees.

11. - Manager and distributor.
    or administrator and distributor
    or management of the trust

12. - Comparison of tax-exempt and equivalent taxable
    income.

13. - Taxable equivalent yield table.

* 14. - Purchase of shares. (How to)
    Purchase by wire.
    Purchase by check.

MUTUAL FUNDS-- They're quiet giants in the world of investing.

* 15. - Shareholder investment account—These are the services.
 Redemptions of shares
 Check redemption
 Regular redemption
 Expedited redemption
 Retirement plans
 Systematic investing
 Systematic withdrawal plan
 Tax sheltered retirement plan
 Monthly distribution plan
 Automatic investment of dividends and distributions
 Automatic withdrawals
 Reinvestment privilege
 Transfer
 Keogh plans

* 16. - Determination of net asset value.

 17. - Distributions and tax information.

* 18. - Portfolio transactions and brokerage.

* 19. - Portfolio list of investments.

 20. - Investment adviser.

 21. - Suitability for investors. (Money Market Funds)

 22. - Voting rights.
 Reports to shareholders.

 23. - Reinvestment privilege.

* 24. - Custodian for transfer, and dividend disbursing agent.

 25. - Writing listed options.
 (Growth Funds) Puts and Calls for hedging.

* 26. - Statement of changes in net assets.
(from last year)

* 27. - Statement of Assets and liabilities.

* 28. - Statement of operations.

* 29. - Notes to financial statements

30. - Appendix
Money Market—commercial paper ratings.
Municipals—Bond ratings
Writing listed options
Growith funds—Puts and Calls for hedging.

31. - General information.

32. - Independent Auditor's report.

MUTUAL FUNDS - FOR THE SERIOUS INVESTOR.

The following are explanations of the more important segments of the prospectus, and they are numbered to relate to the list of chapter headings of the prospectus which have already been enumerated.

#5. - Investment objectives and policies.
This section of the prospectus will satisfy one of your prime concerns which is the fund's purpose. It will tell you what their long range plans are for your investment. These plans may be for growth, income, or a combination of income and stability.

This section will also reveal the fund's goal and what its main thrust or emphasis will be to achieve this goal; how they will tailor their portfolio. Additionally, this section of the prospectus will tell what the fund's main type of security will be in its formation of the portfolio, and whether it will be common stocks, preferred stocks, or bonds; and the relative ratio of importance they intend to place on the various types of securities they will buy. Funds will also sometimes indicate the risk exposure they intend to accept; whether it be minimal, average, or above average. Also, by disclosure here of their selling policy, investors may become aware of the dominant tone of this fund. Investors will thereby know if the tone is stable, balanced, or greatly volatile.

#2. - Per share income and capital changes.

This section of the prosepctus is perhaps the second most important for many investors, as it outlines its figures of performance since the formation of the fund.

ARE YOU DEMANDING ENOUGH?

One should become acquainted with a fund's performance, and keeping in mind the type of fund and the investment policy—look at its rating, and if it has a high rating, this fund's performance should be compared with other highly rated performance funds before making a buy decision.

The performance comparison here could be a counterpart of the comparison that an investor would make if he were buying stocks outright. He would then naturally get into comparing his prospective buy stock with the performance being turned in by other companies of the same size and industry. In comparing—depending on the type of fund, one would want to assess the various changes in net asset value from year to year. Also, the dividends distributions, and realized capital gains should come under close scrutiny.

#9. - Investment restrictions.

This section of a prospectus could be considered the third most important section because it outlines the limits of Management's investment function by spelling out a list of restrictive operations in which management may not engage. Many funds have 15 or 20 of these restrictions which the investors should look upon as so many safety valves which help make his investment less speculative. Some of these restrictions forbid management from short selling, buying on margin, borrowing money, buying other than authorized assets, underwriting securities, lending monies, mortgaging fund securities, buying commodities or commodities futures, investing in other investment companies beyond the percentage allowed, investing beyond the percentage allowed for that particular fund in any one industry or type of stock. (Percentages vary.)

VALUE! THE DIFFERENCE BETWEEN WHAT YOU PAY AND WHAT YOU RECEIVE

Municipal funds and tax free money funds would perhaps be restricted to the buying of only municipal bonds and notes. Another restriction would be to pledge its assets, or assign or otherwise encumber them in excess of a specified percentage (perhaps 10%). They could not sell real estate or real estate mortgage loans. They could not invest to gain control or management of another company. Funds cannot retain securities in which their officers, directors, or any manager having investment decision making power in the fund beneficially own a certain percentage of a company -- perhaps 1/2 of 1%, or if a group of the above own 5% beneficially. Some funds disallow investments in securities of issuers having less then 3 years of continuous operations. Some funds policies limit the buying of securities which have not been registered under the Securities Act of 1933. Perhaps up to 5% would be allowed. The policies of some funds would forbid the managers from investing fund assets in oil, gas, or mineral exploration programs, (no wildcatting) although the same funds would most probably be permitted to invest in common stocks of companies that invested in, or partially sponsored such programs. Funds may not act as general underwriters of securities, except that they might be deemed to be underwriters under certain Federal Securities laws in connection with the disposition of portfolio securities. Mutual funds are not permitted to issue senior securities under the Investment Company Act of 1940 (no preferred stocks). Most funds would shy away from investments in securities having limiited marketability.

The more speculative fund might have but 4 or 5 restrictive clauses, and some of the above restricitions might very well be considered normal operating procedure for some funds; but these minimum restrictions of course set up an operational tone which would suggest a certain degree of risk in that fund's investment policy.

NO MATTER WHAT YOU DO - CHANCES ARE
THE MUTUALS CAN HELP YOU DO IT BETTER.

#14 Purchase of shares. — (how to)
This segment of a prospectus is important to an investor because it spells out exactly how a potential fundholder may buy into a specific fund. To minimize confusion the investor should learn from this section of a prospectus just what is required in the way of an initial investment, and what are the subsequent purchase payments. Most of the prospectusses are mailed along with an application blank. All materials from the fund should be read with care by the potential investor. He should be sure that he understands before signing, just what type of account he is opening. Is the plan a voluntary (open account) one which is subject to change at the pleasure of the investor?

You may very well be signing up to a front-load (contractual) plan which you might intend to avoid. With this plan of course a large portion of your first year's purchases into the fund may go into sales commissions. The high commission payment up-front has the essential effect of reducing considerably the amount of your initial investment which can immediately be invested profitably in your favor. The effect for example of a 8 1/2 % front-load commission on a $10,000 investment would be to reduce the working investment by $850. Now we're looking at an investment of $9,150 instead of a $10,000 one. We're also looking at a front-load percentage of nearly 9.3% of the invested capital.

This section of the prospectus may explain how the price of a fund share is arrived at, and may give the per-share sales charge. Some of the funds have a reduced sales charge as the amount invested increases, and these funds will show a percentage table outlining how the sales charge drops as the amount invested rises. One should be especially aware of the charge described as "the sales charge as a percentage of the amount invested". This is the percentage which reduces your actual productive investment.

MUTUAL FUNDS - WHY SETTLE FOR LESS

This table will be especially evident in the prospectus of a fund such as a high yeilding municipal fund with a high initial investment requirement of perhaps $1,000 to $2,500, and where initial investments from institutions might run as high as a million dollars. This prospectus section will also tell the investor who to contact for an initial purchase; whether it be any broker, a specific broker or distributor, or the fund itself. The purchase price of fund shares is normally the net asset value determined at the time the order is received by the fund. The net asset figure arrived at on a specific day would be the cost of fund shares sold to an investor on that specific day. Any investor orders arriving at the fund after the close of the New York Stock Exchange on any given day would carry the net asset value calculated on the next day that the exchange is open.

One should bear in mind that even in buying into no-load funds, investors may in some cases buy through their registered broker-dealers who will most likely charge a fee (not a commission) for their service as the fund's intermediary. If you're one of those people who are well intentioned buy not very disciplined in carrying out your intended investment plans, take heart; for many funds have a good service which permits fundholders to make regualr purchases of their fund's shares by using pre-authorized checks drawn against the fundholder's bank account. Like automatic bank deposit in reverse (one way to profitably reduce that stashed away money).

#15. - Shareholder investment account.
The redemption of fund shares under the "Shareholder Investment Account" list previously shown is also a very important segment of the prospectus. The procedures for redemption of shares are very similar from fund to fund. However, there may be variations and especially as concerns the different type funds such as from regular stock funds to money market funds, or from municipal and public utility funds.

THE MORE YOU KNOW ABOUT MUTUAL FUNDS THE MORE YOU'LL UNDERSTAND WHY INVESTORS DEPEND ON THEM.

Shares of a fund may be redeemed for cash at any time at the current net asset value per share next determined after the request for redemption is received in good order by the fund, in care generally of its transfer agent. Good order generally means that the requests to redeem shares must include the following documentation:

(1) The stock certificates if they were issued originally at the time of purchase by the holder.

(2) A letter of instructions, or a stock power assignment which specifies the number of shares or the dollar amount to be redeemed, signed by all the registered owners of such shares in the exact names in which they are registered.

(3) A guarantee of the signature of each registered owner by a commercial bank, a trust company, or a member broker of a domestic stock exchange.

(4) Other necessary legal documents, if required, such as: in the case of estates, guardianships, trusts, custodianships, corporations, and possibly pension and profitsharing plans.

If you are not certain as to the requirements for redemption, you should consult with your fund for details. The redemption dollar amount may be more or less than the shareholder's cost depending on the market value of the fund's portfolio of securities as of the next close of the New York Stock Exchange on the day of redemption. The redemption payment will be made within seven days after the tender unless there is a purchase check being cleared for the fund, in which case a redemption payment check could take ten days or even longer until the transfer agent for the fund is satisfied that the payment for the customer's outstanding purchase has or will be collected.

SECURITIES
THE KIND OF STUFF
THAT MUTUAL FUNDS
ARE MADE OF

INCORPORATED UNDER THE LAWS OF THE STATE OF CALIFORNIA, MARCH 19, 1931

SOUTHWEST GAS CORPORATION

THIS CERTIFICATE IS TRANSFERABLE IN LAS VEGAS OR IN THE CITY OF NEW YORK

PUGET SOUND POWER & LIGHT COMPANY

— THE STATE OF WASHINGTON

NOT MORE THAN 100,000 SHARES

SN 141513

SN141513

INCORPORATED UNDER THE LAWS OF
THE COMMONWEALTH OF PENNSYLVANIA

SHARES
100

THIS CERTIFICATE IS TRA
IN PITTSBURGH, PA; NEW Y

CUSIP 264228

DUQUESNE LIGHT COMPANY

FULLY PAID

COMMON STOCK
WITHOUT ANY NOMINAL
OR PAR VALUE

INCORPORATED UNDER THE LAWS
OF THE STATE OF TEXAS

GULF STATES UTILITIES

THIS IS TO
CERTIFY   JOSEPH J VILLENEUVE & DELORES VILLENEUVE
THAT   JT TEN

Reading The Bond Tables

Closed at 810 - Off 1 1/2 or $15.00. Every 1 represents $10.00

2 Here Represents 2. $1000 Bonds

Current Yield Trading at Current Discount Price of 81 or $810.

Selling at a Premium $1080 for a 1000 Bond

BOND			CUR. YLD.	VOL.	HIGH	LOW	CLOSE	NET CHG.
WIDGETS INC.	7 3/4	94	9.6	2	81	81	81	-1 1/2
WIDGETS INC.	8 1/2	16	11.	163	79 3/4	79	79 1/4	+1 1/4
GISMO INC.	8 S	98	8.5	6	94 1/2	94 1/2	94 1/2	-1/2
JUNKET INC.	4 1/2 S	92	CV	18	108	104 1/2	108	+5 1/2
BIG BUY INC.	9 5/8	19	11.	40	89 1/2	89 1/4	89 1/2	+2

Yield Percent to Maturity Date of 2019

Maturing in 1998

89 1/2 - Short Representation of $895.

Net Change from Yesterday is $55.00

Maturing in the Year 2019

Convertible Bond

Explanations:

The first column from left to right is the firm name or abbreviation of the firm's name. Next to the name of the company would be a full number or a mixed number such as 7 3/4 or 7 This is the interest rate on the bond which the company will pay until maturity date.

The 7 3/4 would be followed immediately by the maturity date, which in the case of "Widgets Inc. " above is 94 shortened from the year 1994. If the reading after the name read as follows: 9s 12, the s following the nine percent is merely a plural expression, (nines) and the maturity date would be the year 2012. And it follows that a showing of 9 1/2s 6 would indicate an interest rate of 9 1/2% to the maturity date of 2006.

In the above illustration the Widgets 7 3/4 interest rate is on a $1000.00 bond, because all bonds in these tables represent $1000.00 bonds to maturity date. Every point in the net change column represents $10.00 and every fraction of a point represents a fraction of $10.00.

Current Yield:

Current yield is just what the term implies, current yield but not necessarily on the $1000.00 value, but on the current market value which represents the bond as being discounted, or as being currently sold at a premium (or over the $1000.00 figure) in the **secondary** market.

Current yield is a percentage figure. The illustration above shows the bonds of (fictitious) Widgets Inc. which carry a 7 3/4% return to maturity date closing for the day at 81 or $810.00. The current yield of 9.6% was obtained by dividing 81 into 7 3/4.

Current yield is possibly the most difficult figure to understand about bonds. This misunderstanding may be overcome if one considers that in the face of generally rising interest rates many bond holders holding long term low interest rate bonds may elect to sell their $1000.00 bond at, shall we say $810.00 (or at a discount). They would then use this same money to buy current high interest bonds with the strategy of more than overcoming the loss of $190.00 on the sale of the old bonds. The new buyer of the old bonds discounted to $810.00 not only enjoys the old interest rate, but in effect improves his return because his interest rate will be figured on his cost which is $810.00 instead of $1000.00. Hence the **current** yield of 9.6%.

The reverse occurs when current interest rates start touching below the levels of maturity interest rates. In this trading climate bonds will sell at premium prices (over $1000.00 each, or over par).

Premium is simply the excess of the current market price over par value (or redemption value) which in the case of most bonds is $1000.00

In the bond table illustration we find that "Junket Inc." convertible bonds closed at a premium price of 108 (or $1080). If the "Junket" convertible feature on this $1000.00 bond is 40 shares of the common at $25.00 a share, there would financially be no point in converting, as the bond interest would most probably be higher than the common stock dividend. However, if the common was to go up to $30.00 a share, a $200.00 profit could be made on the conversion, hence investors would pay the premium on the bonds of "Junket Inc." while the common stock was moving from $25.00 to the $30.00 level. There are 2 very important things to remember about the last 5 columns of the bond table illustration, and these are: #1-every unit in the volume column represents a $1000.00 bond and #2-every unit in the 4 right hand columns—high, low, close, and net change represents $10.00. Hence 81 would be read as $810.00, and 5 1/2 net change would be read as $55.00.

Defaults in bond issues are **rare events**, which means that the bond buyers will get their principal back plus interest if the bonds are held to maturity. Hence, there is vey little risk for those holding on until the maturity date.

The current price of bonds at any given time is highly dependent on the "yo-yo" up and down action of **interest rates**. Some 40 to 50 years ago interest rates were very steady, and this stability prompted most investors to hold the bonds to maturity. While many people in those days held these bonds for the full term, they were perhaps justified in believing that long term, these were a better investment than a bank account.

Today! it's a different "ball game." With so many investment vehicles available, and so many big money ventures coming of age, investors want to be **more liquid** to enable them to **participate** in the event that interest rates rise drastically, thus enabling them to buy the newer bonds carrying the higher interest rates; or, if a bull market is developing in stocks, many bond buyers become sellers to participate in that stock market up-tic, thus gathering for themselves some **good quick capital gains**. When interest rates rise there is a strong downward pressure placed on the older bonds which command a lower interest rate to maturity.

You can therefore bet your "sweet patootee" that investors will then not buy a 5% or 6% bond at par if current interest rates are now 10% to 12%. The old 5% or 6% bonds would have to be **discounted drastically** to currently sell in the higher rate setting on the over-the-counter market; but once the bond has been pounded down (discounted) to the right level, it will be competitive with the higher paying bond's percentage of return. In this case the old $1,000 bond at 5% would have the same percentage of return of the new bond if the old one was discounted at $500. One must therefore think of bond prices as **reacting inversely** to the changes in interest rates.

The question of **quality** is the key factor in buying bonds. Unlike stocks where several or many factors enter in to the decision making process to buy or refrain from buying; bonds are purchased based on their quality that is intensively researched by the rating services. There are hundreds of bonds of equal quality on the market at any one time, so it's relatively easy to arrive at a buy decision. Quality-wise a conservative investor should confine his or her purchase to **investment quality bonds** which carry the rating of AAA, AA, A, and BBB.

The bond market is by far the largest of markets, and in terms of money changing hands the stock market is a **dwarf** by comparison. With over 50,000 issues changing hands on any given day, it's easy to see that the availability of bonds is so great that there is **no need** to go after **specific company bonds**.

The second consideration for the average investor in buying bonds is the pricing structure. In buying a 20 year AAA rated municipal bond one might be required to pay $1150. However, if one were to sell that same bond on that particular day, it perhaps would not bring more than $1050 to the seller—the spread being 100 dollars. Hence the need to shop around with several brokers to **reduce this spread** if one is selling. On shorter terms bonds of 10 to 12 years maturity the spread would be much lower.

In building a bond portfolio, investors should look for the **highest quality bonds**, the highest interest rate consistent with the high quality, and if a large investment is involved, **diversification** is important to help insulate the bondholder against those wide **interest rate swings**, and essentially safe-guard the principal in a more liquid setting more conducive to coping with the occasional set-backs which occasionally prevail in this market.

The **way to go** for most people would be by way of the bond **mutual funds** where it is relatively easy to buy and sell mutual fund shares. While the minimum investment in the average bond fund might be $1,000 and would perhaps buy the investor a share in 75 to 200 different bonds; the minimum investment required by most brokers on a municipal bond would be $5,000.

MUTUAL FUNDS - THEY'VE GOT WHAT YOU NEED TO SUCCEED.

With a bond fund you know precisely what you are buying, and there's no need to **examine the issues**, the quality, size, and tax ramifications. These items are all researched and acted upon by **the funds**.

Selling mutual bond fund shares is **very easy**. With some funds the selling may be done by simply making a **phone call**. There is a **designated price** at which a sell transaction can be made everyday. If the bond fund is of the **no load variety**, the buy and sell prices are the same. However, selling a **specific bond** can be complicated, cumbersome, and often-times quite costly.

One should buy bonds only if they **fit-in** with one's investment objectives. It's important to understand what you're buying before you get involved. When buying bonds you're actually **loaning** your hard earned **money** to an entity, either governmental or corporate, that has issued the bond. You know **precisely** how much you will receive if you **hold** the bond to maturity. You receive interest for the company's use of your money and , at maturity you'll receive the principal amount you originally invested, plus any accured interest.

However, interest rate swings of the last several years have made bonds less stable, and more of an **active trading vehicle**; as bond prices move in the opposite direction of interest rates. In an environment of fast moving interest rates, it's very possible to sustain losses if one sells out prior to the maturity date.

With many investors the most popular bonds are those issued by the United States Treasury. These are considered to be absolutely safe by most investors. The next category would be the **corporate bond sector**. These are given a rating by the 2 largest national rating services, and ranked based on the **credit worthiness** of the company at the time that the bonds are issued; and the rankings are amended up or down from time to time as the **viability** of the issuing company changes.

The third major bond catagory would be the **municipal bonds**. These are tax exempt bonds of states, municipalities, or other governmental subdivisions that are ranked according to the **community's credit rating** based on such things as its taxation base—or other sound income base such as highway tolls in the case of a toll Highway Commission bond.

Aside from the above bonds are the **mortgage-backed** bonds which return more than the Treasury yields, but are apt to be **called in** for early redemption.

The zero coupon treasury bonds are **drastically discounted**, but interest is not paid out periodically such as other bonds. These are sometimes called "treasury strips" becuse they are stripped of their coupon, buy redeemed at face value which is drastically higher than the original cost value for any specified face value and term of maturity. The buying prices of zeroes are determined by the bond's interest rate on the date the purchase is made.

The cost of a $10,000 face value zero, maturing in 12 years might only cost about $3,500. One might consider the difference of $6,500 as one's interest. These zero bonds may be purchased in denominations as small as $1,000.

The main disadvantage of zeroes is that the I.R.S. demands that on taxable accounts the tax in each year's **accrued value** has to be paid just as if the bondholder had received an **interest check**. You're thereby paying taxes in **advance** of **receiving your return**. For this reason the main beneficiaries of zeroes are perhaps the I.R.A. accounts, Keoghs, and various other pension accounts where the bond return is tax-deferred.

Unlike zero coupon treasury bonds which are purchased at **deep discounts**, the straight treasuries are bought at **face value** and redeemed at face value if held to the maturity date. In the meantime they pay **coupon interest** twice a year, thus providing the bondholder with an ongoing **interest income**. However, as no discount is applied to the purchase of **straight treasuries** one may easily see that the initial investment is much greater than that of the zero treasury bond. Thinking in terms of quality it would seem that an investor trying to build a bond portfolio would want to build in at least a **60% proportion** of those bonds that carry a triple A, double A, or straight A rating.

**Bonds are the
income producing
segment
of the market.**

Bond:

A bond is essentially an IOU or promissory note of a corporation. These are usually issued in $1000.00 units. A bond is legal evidence of a debt on which the issuing company promises to pay the bond holder a specific interest rate for a specific length of time, and to repay this loan or IOU on the expiration date. The bond holder is a creditor of a corporation, and not an owner as in the case of a shareholder (or stockholder).

Debenture:

A debenture is a long-term debt of a corporation that is generally secured by the assets and general credit standing of the company, rather than by a mortgage.

A debenture may either be a bond or a preferred stock having prior preference over all other preferred or common issues. Debentures can realistically be called "junior grade bonds."

Registered Bond:

A registered bond is one which is registered on the books of the issuing company in the name of the bond owner. Transfer can only occur when the bond is endorsed by the registered owner.

Coupon Bonds:

These bonds have interest coupons attached. The coupons are clipped from the bonds and turned in for payment by the corporation as the interest paying periods become due.

Income Bonds:

Income bonds usually promise to repay principal but to pay interest only when it is earned. In certain cases the unpaid interest on an income bond may accumulate and be considered as a claim against the company when the bond comes due. Some income bonds are also issued as a substitute for preferred stock. These bonds are normally traded flat—(or without interest).

Mortgage Bond:

This is a bond that is secured by a mortgage on a property.

Municipal Bond:

A bond issued by a political subdivision such as a state, county, city, town or village. State mandated authorities, and agencies may also issue such bonds. Generally the interest income from such bonds is exempt from federal income taxes.

Serial Bonds:
This is a bond issue maturing in comparatively small amounts at pre-stated intervals.

General Mortgage Bonds:
These bonds are secured by an overall mortgage on the corporation's property, but they are often outclassed priority-wise by one or perhaps several other mortgages.

Guaranteed Bonds:
These bonds have interest or principal, or both guaranteed by another company. The company which guarantees is usually a subsidiary.

Collateral Trust Bond:
This bond is secured by collateral which is deposited with a trustee. The collateral may be various securities, or quite often the collateral consists of stocks or bonds of companies owned or controlled by the issuing company.

Government Bonds:
These obligations of the U.S. Government are generally regarded as the highest grade of all the bonds.

Convertible:
This is a bond, debenture, or preferred share of stock which may be exchanged by the owner for common stock or some other security, according to the terms and conditions of the issue.

Face Value:
This is the value of the bond appearing on the face of the bond, usually $1000.00 unless otherwise specified by the issuing corporation (also called par value).

Face value is generally the amount the issuing firm promises to pay at maturity. Face value (or par value) does not change, and is not to be mistaken for current market value.

Sinking Fund:
This is money that is regularly set aside by a corporation to redeem its bonds or preferred stock at various time intervals as specified in the Charter of Incorporation, or bond indenture.

Callable:
A bond issue which may be redeemed in full or in part under pre-determined conditions by the issuer before the maturity date. Preferred shares may also be retired under similar conditions.

Flat:
When trading in bonds this term is used to indicate that the purchase price of the bonds includes consideration for all the unpaid accruals of interest. Bonds which are in default of a principal or interest, and income bonds are usually traded "flat."

Junior Bonds:
These bonds are secondary to other issues. In the event of company foreclosure the Junior Bond claims will be satisfied only after all prior claims of the senior bonds have been met.

Accrued Interest:
The accumulation of interest on a bond since the last payment of interest was made. The buyer of the bond usually pays the market price plus accrued interest earned on the bond since the most recent coupon payment.

Coupons:
These are small segments of the bond certificate representing interest for various six-month periods. A bond maturing in 20 years would have 40 perforated segments which are detached every 6 months for the collection of interest due.

Commercial Paper:
These are IOU's or certificates issued by corporations to raise money for short term, usually less than 270 days.

Primary and Secondary:
A primary offering is the first marketing effort to sell a new stock or bond issue. This sale is generally conducted by a syndicate of investment bankers who buy or underwrite the new issue. This banking group then serves as a wholesaler, re-selling the issue to the general public through their sales organization. A "secondary" would be the sale of an additional large block of bonds or stock, which adds to and therefore dilutes the primary offering.

Another expression— buying in the secondary market would simply mean buying in an existing open market, (the auction, or over-the-counter) following completion of the original issue.

"It's the talk of the town."

BLACK MONDAY CATASTROPHE— AND PROGRAM TRADING:

Castastrophe is part of all of our lives at some time or other. The markets are no different. During the period of a person's lifetime there will also be several disasters in the market places. One of the gravest crisis ever to hit the world's financial markets occurred on **October 19th and 20th** of 1987.

Prior to the debacle of Oct. 19th the markets experienced a five year **major bull market** that seemed unstopable until a few weeks before Oct. 19th, when stock prices started to decline amid increasingly dramatic market swings. With general concerns in this country and aboard over the country's **trade** and **budget deficits, interest rates,** and the acceleration of naval operations in the Persian Gulf; a negative **mob psychology** is generally thought to have developed among larger investor groups, and these are said to be the investor feelings which culminated in to the **panic selling** sprees of Oct. 19th and 20th.

A **confidence crisis** of such magnitude developed on Black Tuesday Oct. 20th, 1987 that stocks, options, and futures trading just about came to halt, as some of the largest company stocks could not sold for the lack of buyers. The Industrial Average was **ineffective** as a trading tool because many of its stocks were not trading. The **big board specialists** whose function it is to **stabilize** the market by trading for their own account to keep the trading gap narrow, were overwhelmed by their unfilled customer sell orders after many of them had lost millions of dollars trying to stem the tide of selling orders by buying to support prices.

Monday October 19th 1987 has been dubbed **Black Monday**. On that day the Dow Jones Industrial Average plunged 508 points to compile its **largest loss ever**. This heart wresting market loss on that Monday, set up the stage for **Black Tuesday** which was considered by many to be the most danger-

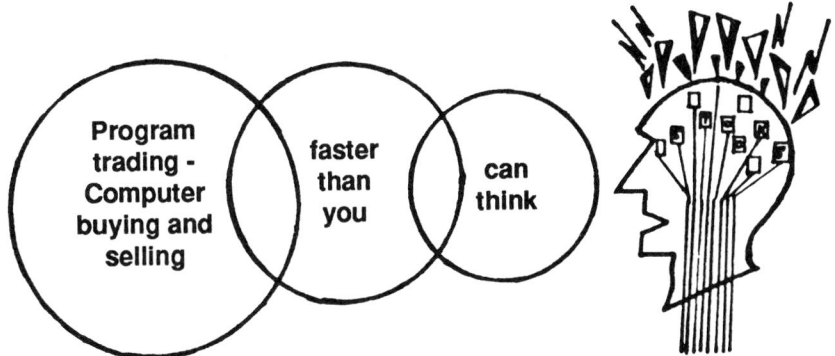

ous day that Wall Street has suffered for perhaps some 50 years. We're talking about a bad day crunch that cost roughly 500 billion dollars in consumer wealth.

The elusive question that is difficult to understand is why this massive collapse occurred on these **specific days** of October 19th and 20th. There's no doubt that the collapse was inevitable if one considers the many factors that seemed to jell and jam as if they were **thoughtfully contrived** to bring about a specific result.

A prime source of selling pressure came from **portfolio insurance** money **managers**. These people seek to insure pension funds against the ravages of bear markets by selling futures, or options matched to indexes such as the Standard & Poor's 500 index. This strategy is intended to relieve the pension fund's concern over the downturns of their long term stock holdings. This brings us to Program Trading that is loosely defined as a **super-fast means** of the buying and selling of **clusters** (or baskets) of **stocks**, very often by the way of the Big Board's high-speed **Super Dot** trading system.

Program trading has become a great way for institutions to make **very rapid changes** in their portfolios. The controversial aspect of Program Trading centers on **index arbitrage**. This combines the buying and selling of stocks, and at the same time generating offsetting trades in stock-index futures. the traders using this strategy normally look for **small price gaps** between the stocks and futures. They then buy whichever stock or future is cheaper, and sell which ever is the more expensive.

These index arbitrage players monitor their **computer screens** continuously; always on the alert of course for the **difference** between stock and futures index prices. When the **spread** between the two of these widens or

"Standard & Poor's 100" and "Standard & Poor's 500" are Registered Trademarks of Standard & Poor's Corporation.

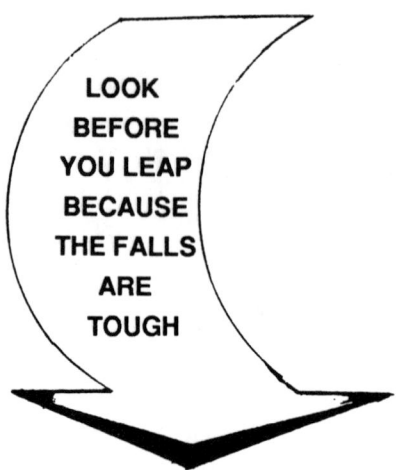

LOOK
BEFORE
YOU LEAP
BECAUSE
THE FALLS
ARE
TOUGH

shrinks enough, the arbitrager will use the big board Super Dot system to punch out trades that will take from a few seconds to perhaps five minutes for completion; and we're talking about a trade that may involve 25 to perhaps 50 million dollars. This type of trading can send prices gyrating and may scare the living hell out of many a trader and investor!

That dreadful October 19th held many surprises, as a full blown crisis of confidence seemed to panic investors into selling whatever securities they held. The largest mutual fund family was deluged by selling calls from their equity customers who **wanted out**. The immediate call for these equity fund **redemptions** made upon this largest of funds, having in excess of 100 portfolios was so great that the fund was reportedly forced into selling nearly a billion dollars worth of equities to meet the redemptions of stock-fund shares, and to accomodate the heavy volume of switches into money market funds.

Two of the largest pension funds at this time unloaded **several billion dollars** in equities on that Black Monday. The Chrysler Corporation's $3.6 billion pension fund is reported to have unloaded 500 million in stocks adding more fuel to this "blazing fire" sell-off. During the previous week-end the Maryland State Pension plan had announced that it was shifting 2.3 billion from stocks in to the bond markets. The pension funds in this country own about 25% of all equities, or roughly 2 trillion dollars worth; so, it's no wonder that there was concern about the safety of their stock holdings.

Also, block traders who are employed by Wall Street's most famous brokerage houses became very vigilant, as they sold out positions just as

DON'T PUT
ALL YOUR
EGGS IN
ONE BASKET
-- DIVERSIFY

fast as they were forced to buy them from their clients, thus maintaining the **customer goodwill**, but placing **more** stress pains on the markets.

While most mutual funds were only **moderate traders** on Black Monday, the foreign institutions came in with some heavy stock selling. Some of the bank trust departments sold stocks heavily, for the safer haven of government bonds.

Black Monday October 19, 1987 was the **worst day ever** for the Big Board's specialists. This group of some 50 little known but powerful companies are bound by the Big Board's rules which require that they buy and sell their assigned stocks during **volatile times** to keep order in the market place. The specialists will buy stocks when no one else will, and they sell stocks from their inventories when none is available to a buyer. Therefore, in normal times the specialists provide the **last bulwark** of **liquidity** for the investor.

As the markets "skidded southward" on that Monday the specialists **bore** the **brunt** of the fall, trying desperately to **impede** this irresistible force—this juggernaut of sales pressure which was occuring in the absence of investor buying. The Big Board specialists were in a state of total desperation by the afternoon of Black Monday, as they had tried in vain to stem the onslaught of **investor selling** by using about 2 billion dollars of their monies in fruitless attempts to **stabilize prices**, and nothing seemed to work. Everyone seemed "hell bent" on trying to somehow crawl into that invisible "black hole" that wasn't there, by **selling** in **desperation** to avoid their anticipated losses.

BLACK TUESDAY MELTDOWN:

After the drubbing that the markets took on Black Monday, **credit dollars** for the Big Board specialists became a big problem as they clamored for more unsecured "big bucks" from their banking sources who sensed great problems developing as they put the final squeeze on the specialists, **cutting off** their millions of dollars which they were routinely accustomed to borrowing for the **simple asking**.

Enter the Fed.— After "fast track" and **agonizing** discussions between "market big wigs", the White House officials, and the Federal Reserve Officials, the decision was made that the Fed. would end the credit squeeze foisted upon the Big Board specialists by **committing itself** to serve as a source of liquidity to support the economic and financial system. The Federal Reserve opened liquidity by flooding the banking system with dollars. The banks were told at that time that they would be kept liquid, thus enabling them to support the needed **infusion of capital** so necessary to accommodate the millions needed by the specialist's firms if they were to serve as an important source of liquidity for the markets.

When the specialist's cash millions had been "tapped out" on Black Monday, one may well imagine their surprise at suddenly being cut off of the **necessary credit** at the New York banks where they routinely borrowed uncollaterized millions on a daily basis.

When the Big Board opened on that Tuesday, many specialists refused to open trading until enough buy orders were in to allow the shares to trade on the up-side. When stock prices recovered somewhat and were mostly up, the major investment firms and the specialists sped up their unloading process, dumping large inventories, which again dried up demand **causing the meltdown** whereby some of the most important stocks broke down and could not be traded to the "absent buyers". The program traders and portfolio insurers who seemed so destructive on that Monday, were virtually absent on Tuesday.

While this was going on at the Big Board, the over-the-counter trading was also in such disarray that **market makers** stopped answering the phones for lack of buy orders.

SOME SPECULATION IS PRESENT IN BUYING ANY STOCK -- but speculation can be found in most everything we do.

By midday on Black Tuesday (Oct. 20,1987) the markets were in such **confusion** that most futures and options trading had come to a standstill, and there was even talk of closing the Big Board market. While this **near meltdown** uncertainty was being felt on all major markets, a highly unusual event was starting up at the **Major Market Index** futures of the Chicago Board of Trade. An extraordinary rally was staged in the Major Market Index futures contracts pushing the index to a healthy premium of the underlying cash value of the index. This set the **stage** for heavy buying on the markets of these **Blue Chip stocks** which are a reflection of the Dow; as most of the stocks in the MMI index are essentially those of the Dow Jones Industrial Average.

The markets had been so undersold by midday of Black Tuesday that certain investment bankers seized upon this opportunity to get some buying action going. These bankers called upon corporate **chief executives** throughout the country, egging them on to buy back some of their company's stock. This two pronged maneuver of **corporate buy backs**, along with the **strong rally** of the Major Market Index shown above, were perhaps the two factors that saved the day and probably the entire stock arena setting; as the volume on the big board responded by skyrocketing to an unprecedented 608 million shares. This volume was slightly higher than Black Monday, and roughly three times the normal daily volume.

Six months after the crisis of Black Monday and Tuesday, stock markets were still experiencing daily volumes in **very low ranges**, like 160 million shares daily, and the profits from index arbitrage was **shrinking rapidly** for the securities firms.

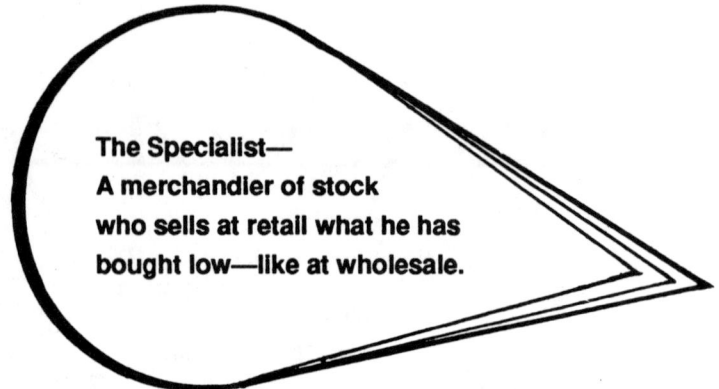

The Specialist—
A merchandler of stock
who sells at retail what he has
bought low—like at wholesale.

Meanwhile, big pressures and scrutinies are being applied to the industry by both the big board and the House Energy and Commerce Finance Sub-Committee, with the idea of developing measures to control **program trading** in **index futures**, thus ultimately making the trading of stocks more palatable to the masses of investors.

While the facts seem to indicate that the general public was "**creamed**" on Oct. 19th and 20th of 1987, this same general public will perhaps not be anxious to return into a market the prices of which do not reflect the **economy**, or **earnings reports**; but rather are reflective of a selfish strategy tool that sends waves of computer-generated selling or buying prices whipping up and down yo-yo style, to the astonishing pullback of the **traders**, and many of the **long term players**.

It's ironic that the industry has computerized systems capable of making **so much money**; yet when abused, this same technology will cause enough turmoil to cost the industry **billions of dollars** if it neglects the best interest of the masses of the players. At this writing there is a great division that is occuring especially at the **regional firms** where the retail brokers are lining up against the program trading operations of the **large national firms.** The result should be interesting.

Don't
overlook
the **mob**
psychology
of **the**
market place

THE NUTS AND BOLTS OF WALL STREET
IS INFORMATION --
KNOW HOW TO USE IT.

PROGRAM TRADING:

Program trading is a relatively new practice since the advent of the computer, using computer programs to buy or sell stocks. These progroms are devised so that certain chosen securities (sometimes called **clusters** or baskets of stocks) are purchased or sold electronically when the prices reach a **pre-designated** level. This method of trading has now come under great scrutiny of the authorities; because, the tremendous volume of stock shares traded via the **Superdot** trading system is being blamed in great measure for the stock market **meltdown** of prices that occurred on Oct.19th and 20th of 1987.

As market prices rise or fall beyond the **parameters** set by the program, the stocks in the programs are purchased or sold at an alarming rate of speed. This engenders added sympathetic trading within the same trend set by the computer trades and the result is occasionally an **explosion** of trades. Investors and many institutional traders don't like program trading because even though these trades are currently allowed, they are analogous to **bear raiders** selling short to drive the market down, whose practice is prohibited by the Securities and Exchange Commission.

Today, there are strict laws to prevent price manipulation, and investors are looking for **protection** from the ravages of program trading which is a form of **price manipulation** not currently covered by S.E.C. rules. This could change if the practice continues.

Portfolio insurance program trades were perhaps the biggest culprits in activating the **huge sell off** of Oct.19th of 1987. These are programs that were designed to help **institutional investors**, especially the hugh pension funds, from losing excessively in declining markets. In the situation of Oct.19, the portfolio insurance programs actually triggered the massive selling drive that resulted in destroying the markets on that bleak Black Monday.

The value perception of investors makes a market

Some of the experts who have studied this problem believe that the public's perception is no longer that of a **free market**, but of a market that is far too limited to the **rich** and the powerful. These experts believe that this perception, if continued will ultimately destroy public confidence, and especially if **another crash** should occur. Most of this program trading seems to be done by about a dozen large U.S. brokerages for their own account, or for that of some large funds. Trading in this manner, these brokers use techniques that are **unavailable** to the individual investor.

Index arbitrage is that form of program trading that has taken the heaviest criticism. This is the carrying out of blizzards of trades and profiting from **price differences** between stocks and index futures. If continued, program trading only encourages the people who are at the big trading houses to try shaving profits here and there on a daily basis at the expense of Mr. and Mrs. average investor.

Another trading abuse that the authorities seem to be focusing on, is that of intermarket **front-running** that involves trading in futures contracts in order to profit from knowledge of upcoming orders in the stock market. This is just another market **manipulation** that further serves to erode public confidence. Certain abuses in the stock markets seem to go on for years—it takes a **crisis** though, such as the debacle of Black Monday to somehow start a **purging process** that may in time enable the markets to clean up their "dirty linens", hopefully restoring public confidence.

EVERY
STOCKMARKET
HAS ITS DAY -- DON'T
OVERSTAY YOUR
WELCOME.

DISMEMBERMENT OF A MARKET:

A year and a half after the stock market crash of Oct. 19, 1987, a dismal gloom has fallen over that traditional bulwark of frenzied energetic motion called the Wall Street **equity trading rooms**. With commission revenues 35% to 50% lower than they were at the time of the crash, people at the block trading desks of most major brokerages are very concerned about **their future** as they ponder the possibility of being subjected to further reductions in staff, to keep that sick bull or bear afloat. I say bull or bear because we still have many people who don't seem to recognize a bull from a bear market.

Meantime, investors both large and small are suffering great anxiety concerning the market's ability to **function normally**. Investors fear that stock prices are responding more to the hidden automated **trading mechanisms** now in use by some of the big institutions; rather than being propelled by the **economic fundamentals** which traditionally have been the market movers.

Before the 1980's, there seemed to be a definite relationship between **economic activity** and the **stock market**. However, during the last six years the market,"cat 'n' mouse fashion" seems to be anticipating illusional **booms and busts** not directly related to the economy. Many believe that this is causing Wall Street to lose its clout as a **predictor** of economic activity.

The communication pipeline to investors seems to be so great, and produce such mixed signals today, that it's no wonder that both large and small investors alike are **traumatized** by this mass of information—some of which could have been a contributing cause of the Oct. 19th disaster.

All that trauma and anxiety out there has more to do with the **soundness** of the markets, rather than the price of stocks. The belief generally shared by many investors that the market is no longer very predictable or stable, may be a factor in the **malaise** of the current markets. Perhaps investors have to start relying more on traditional market moving factors such as: corporate profits, consumer spending, personal income, corporate expansions, changing labor and production markets, and above all, the changing character of those **global business factors** that tend to influence the U.S. economy, by the competitive changes in the international **balance** of **trade**.

The government's Index of Leading Economic Indicators continues to place much weight on the Wall Street industry as a **solid component** of the LEI, even though Wall Street's actual value as a foreteller of economic trends has greatly **diminished**. The markets' accelerated preoccupation with index arbitrage, program trading, and leveraged trading in stock options and futures, are the greedy **speculative functions** which only serve to undermine the market's job as an **allocator** of capital.

Oh yes! let's not forget the **takeover** phenomenon, that occasionally dominates trading activity on the market; yet its contribution to the economy is **very questionable**. The idea of weak, inexperienced managements taking over good well managed companies is certainly repugnant to many investors. Good companies are now becoming the "grab bag" **targets** of corporate **raiders**, who take over good companies, and **plunder** the assets of these companies for their greedy purposes that serve no special **economic good**.

The value of the **money supply** has also become weakened as a factor in the Index of Leading Economic Indicators, as the activity of currency traders increases,while they profit from monetary exchange rate fluctuations. This is an activity that some believe reduces the importance of the money supply as a **solid component** of the **LEI**.

Investors and business tycoons throughout the country use the Index of Leading Economic Indicators as a **valid guide** to taylor their future business plans; but, if the index components are not truly representative of the factors which they supposedly represent, and thereby send out a pattern of **false signals**—this could cost the business world a lot of money, a loss of efficiency, and a weakened **competitive position** worldwide.

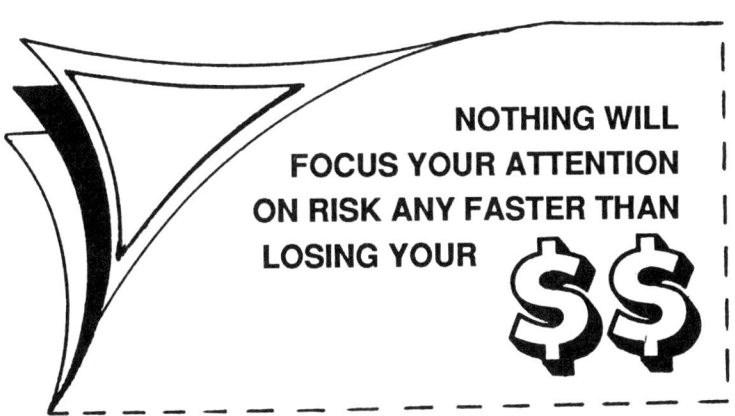

NOTHING WILL
FOCUS YOUR ATTENTION
ON RISK ANY FASTER THAN
LOSING YOUR $$

Since the days of Black Monday and Tuesday, many stocks and bond offerings have been cancelled or postponed, and many corporate buy-out plans have been **scrapped** for fear of **failure**, as individual investors hold back from investing, worried of being trampled of course in a selling stampede reminiscent of the Oct.19th experience.

The selling mania of Oct.19th surely spotlighted the **risks** involved in securities ownership. There's nothing like losing a pot-full of money to focus one's **quick attention on** risk factors, so nobody's betting the farm away these days. Even the institutions, some of which are sitting on **hugh hoards** of **cash**, are itching to invest , but until the markets are more settled, will be pursuing alternative investment.

My suspicion is that one of these days the institutions will get off the sidelines, and again **start competing** with one another for stocks and bonds.

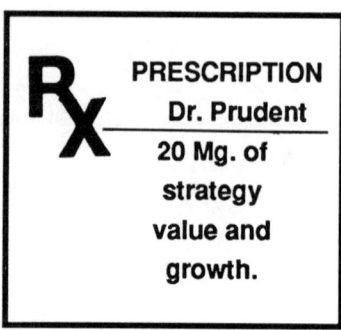

R_X

PRESCRIPTION
Dr. Prudent

20 Mg. of
strategy
value and
growth.

MEDICINE FOR A SICK MARKET:

Reviving a sick market is not always an easy feat. Over a good number of years security markets have had their ups and downs; but none were quite like the disastrous crash of **Oct.19th of '87**. This crash was far reaching and affected all major markets in U.S. and most of those abroad. The Monday morning "quarterbacking" experts attributed all sorts of causes to this phenomenon at the time of the crash. However, the investors, those that fuel the stock markets and were **burned badly** came away with a strong sense of having been snookered by the **program trading** mania—the type of activity whereby clusters of stocks; or, as some would choose to call them baskets of stocks, are traded in a matter of minutes or even seconds.

When these trades come through for execution, they give a **jolt** to the rest of the market creating **gyrations** in stock prices that are perceived as negative. They are perceived as **undesirable** by the average investor because at the time that the many stocks comprising the clusters are traded, investors don't know **what's happening**. A basket of stocks might consist of 50 to 100 million dollars worth of various stocks. When several baskets hit the market simultaneously, whether or not the trades are on the upside or the downside of the market, the resulting furor of **additional buying** or selling activity results in an exaggerated, or **untrue** picture of what should have happened.

When these baskets trade quickly below the market prices as they occasionally do, investors, refusing to be left with a greater loss, will join the selling movement, which just adds to the **selling fury.** These are days in which the Averages should perhaps show a 10 point loss, but because so many independent investors and institutions were intimidated into this **selling frenzy**, the averages might have shown a 25% to perhaps a 48% loss for the day.

WATCH FOR THE FINANCIAL SUPERHIGHWAY

The New York Stock Exchange and three other exchanges are currently in the throws of working hard but separately on their individual version of what some call a **financial Superhighway**, aimed at easing the effects of large trades on the market. These exchanges envision ways of trading big **baskets** of stocks with but a **single buy** or sell order. They hope to **cordon off** these big **institutional** trades from the rest of the market. This is the **"medication"** that the exchanges are prescribing to treat the slow sales fungus that has infected the markets since **Black Monday**. They believe that this approach in the handling of large trades will go a long way toward restoring investor **confidence** generally, in the remaining segment of the market—the retail trade.

It would seem of course that such a plan would improve **liquidity** to the benefit of Mr. and Mrs. average investor. The watchful observers of this injured market believe that some form of basket trading that **bypasses** the **normal channels** will win the regulators' approval. If this happens and the exchanges provide the right kinds of baskets, this could lure a considerable amount of business away from Chicago's futures and options markets. For this reason the Commodities Futures Trading Commission wants to have its **input** into this whole **scenario**. The Commission seems to believe that it should be the federal agency enpowered to review the exchange's basket plans, rather than the S.E.C.. The mechanics of how these clusters of stocks will be offered may be a **critical issue**, especially for the Chicago exchanges that expect to be seriously affected by these proposed newly created innovations.

The final basket plan that gains the regulators' approval may very well be an **accomodation**, or merging of the proposals of two or more of the exchange's ideas. The Standard & Poor's 500 index seems to be highly favored by most of the exchanges as a logical choice for stock baskets; as the S & P 500 is the **benchmark** of professional money managers, and is widely used by **index funds**.

One is occasionally reminded that the post-crash doldrums that followed Black Monday were not necessarily caused by some other kind of investor called a bear; but by a **malaise**—the mere absence of the many bulls that had helped create the pre-crash bull market. For all intents and purposes, when the bulls **stop trading**, they change "ipso facto" into bears. They are then joined by the real market bears, and now you will have a "fait accompli" bear market, even though it's in the best interest of the brokerage business **not to admit** the existence of the bear setting.

Brokerage people look foward to the big **sales volumes** of their glorious bull markets, but they **starve** and go out of business in a disastrous bear market.

Some of the strong brokerage companies have **diversified** their activities, and this tends to cushion their overall losses during periods of strong bearish activity in the markets. Some brokerage firms are heavily into **mutual funds**, where they earn handsome management fees. Some are into **real estate** via the Real Estate Investment Trusts. The brokerage people now want to get into **retail banking** in response to the efforts that banks are currently making to get into the securities business. When a crash occurs, these ancillary business ventures will certainly help the brokerage people with their "**bottom line**".

"Standard & Poor's 100" and "Standard & Poor's 500" are Registered Trademarks of Standard & Poor's Corporation.

The Securities and Exchange Commission

This is the, quasi-judicial agency of the United States whose function it is to administer the federal laws intended to protect the monetary interest of the investing public.

The vigor and health of our nation's economy is highly dependent upon the growth and stability of our commerce and industry which provides employment and a high standard of living to millions, and at the same time generally returns a good profit to the securities of its investors.

The chances for industry to thrive and prosper is greatly dependent upon its ability to obtain finances for plant expansion, research, development, and working capital. The availability of adequate funding for these purposes is highly dependent upon the investing public's confidence in the multitude of sound securities as being safe and profitable mediums for the investment of their savings.

Passage of the Federal Securities Laws was a direct outgrowth of the many abusive practices which had to be dealt with following the stock market crash of 1929.

Adminstration of the Securities Laws on both the national and state levels, along with the more stringent self-policing policies of the securities industry have gone a long way toward re-establishing investor confidence in the essential intregrity ot the securities industry.

With the momentous problems that developed on Oct. 19th and 20th of 1987, more federal and self-regulation of this hugh industry is bound to occur in attempts to eliminate some of the abuses and weakness which in retrospect became so apparent.

Regulation and Enforcement:

The Securities and Exchange Commission is empowered to administer the following federal laws dealing with the regulation of securities: The Securities Act of 1933, The Securities Exchange Act of 1934, The Public Utility Holding Company Act of 1935, The Trust Indenture Act of 1939, and The Investment Company Act of 1940.

These Acts were followed by the 1964 Amendment Acts of Congress after a study had been made of the securities industry by the S.E.C. In 1975 Congress further regulated the securities industry by sweeping revisions called the Securities Reform Act of 1975.

Currently, it looks as if Congress may again be called upon to use its legislative powers to cope with possible current abuses in the high tech aspect of this industry called Program Trading. Another current abuse area seems to be that of insider trading, and especially as it concerns the "takeover" mania.

The Securities Act contains prohibitions against fraud in the sale of securities, whether or not they are registered; and it gives the commission the power to investigate complaints or any other indications of possible fraud, or other illegal activities relative to the sale of securities.

The commission also has the power to initiate federal court actions to enjoin unlawful activities, and it may seek Department of Justice help by referring evidence of fraud, or willful violations with recommendations for criminal prosecution.

INDEX